THE UNFORESEEN

OCCURRENCE

BOOKS BY J. LEE GILBERT

Clown In A Cowboy Hat, 2001

You Can't Judge A Book By It's Cover, 2001

Reflections In Poetry, 2002

THE UNFORESEEN
OCCURRENCE

A TRUE STORY

BY

J. LEE GILBERT

KING AND QUEEN PUBLISHERS, INC.

RICHMOND, VIRGINIA

THE UNFORESEEN OCCURRENCE

Library of Congress Control Number: 2004107382
Cataloging-in-Publication Information may be obtained from the Library of Congress.
ISBN: 0-9714374-3-2
Manufactured in the United States of America
Editor: Jennifer Gilbert
Cover Photography: Gary U. Smith
Cover Illustration: Kelvin Gilbert
Published: April 2005

For more information contact:
King and Queen Publishers, Inc
P. O Box 2037
Glen Allen, Va. 23058
King737@msn.com.

Purchase on line: Barnes&Noble.com
Bordersbooks.com

Bulk orders may be placed with Baker & Taylor Books
Call 1-800-775-1200
First Edition
12345678910

DEDICATION

I dedicate this book to my best friend and wife, Jennifer. She was the person that was there through the lean years picking me up when I would stumble and encouraging me when I was down. As for me, I believe Jennifer is my reward from God for a job well done!

CONTENTS

FOREWORD
By Michael J. Rosner, MD, FACS, PCCM

In these days of lawsuits and rising cost driving physicians out of the practice of medicine and surgery and even worse, deeply into the destructive hold of cynicism, J. Lee Gilbert's story helps balance the equation. This foreword is partly about courage and determination of an individual fighting back from a devastating stroke and it's consequence. It is also about the personal satisfaction, no, joy, experienced by his physicians at his success.

His outcome, largely through his own determination far exceeded the expectations, though not the hopes, of his physicians. J. Lee suffered a cerebral hemorrhage damaging the connections from his eyes to the brain regions where vision is interpreted. His was partially paralyzed. He developed hydrocephalus or water on the brain, further impairing his function and requiring a permanent drainage system (shunt) be placed to reduce the pressure in his head. His memory did not work. He lost the ability to see to the left and also the ability to interpret those few words, which he actually was able to see (alexia) he could not read. This man, who wanted nothing more than to become a poet, had lost the ability to read! This physician never believed for one moment that he would succeed. Hope, yes, believe, no.

Yet J. Lee never gave up. He forced himself to return to work, not one but two jobs. He supported his family through it all. He never gave up his dream to become a published poet. So, in 2001, after nearly twenty years of effort, he published three volumes of his poems. After nearly twenty years of recovery and work - there is no more difficult labor than recovery from a stroke- he now tells the story of accepting the responsibility we have for our families. J. Lee has lived the story and serves as a model for all fathers.

But the story is more that just about fatherhood or family; it is about what can be accomplished by those who do not quit. Who never lose hope. Who do not give up their dreams. It is a story to remind physicians that we must support the efforts of the recovering and not inhibit them. If we do not, then the patient may well fail. If we do, then you can share in the joy and pleasure of his accomplishments, as I do with J. Lee Gilbert.

PREFACE

There is no excuse for a Deadbeat Dad!

During the baby boom generation, the term *Deadbeat Dad* became commonplace. There were several states that in which a *Deadbeat Dad* could escape in order to avoid prosecution and that literally provided safe haven for those who would not live up to their obligation of support. Of course, this left many women and their children on welfare, A.D.C. and other government sponsored programs.

Having reached epidemic proportions, the federal government stepped in and with sweeping legislation cleaned up the program and in all states made it almost impossible for a *Deadbeat Dad* to run from his responsibilities.

However, as proven by this Author, not all fathers choose to neglect their responsibility. From nineteen eighty-seven through nineteen ninety-six, along with two full time jobs, the Author proved to the world it could be done! This book is a testimony to that fact and during those nine and a half years was able to write three very successful poetry books.

Although the ordeal is behind me, the cerebral hemorrhage in nineteen eighty-two; being blind for eleven months and working two full time jobs to clear the state obligation, as stated in my first book, *Clown In A Cowboy Hat,* "Nightmares Are Never Gone".

J. Lee Gilbert

Chapter 1

IN THE BEGINNING

It was a Thursday night in April of 1977 and events that would take place would have a profound effect on my entire future as well as my personality.

As an Elder in the church, I had become very popular and my duties were extremely devotional. It had reached the point that everything I would say was related to Gospel. It seemed as though nothing could be done without my ok or my own involvement in the Church.

Although there was a body of Elders, most of them were complacent and sitting back allowing me to run the show, as it were, and not doing any more than to just get by. Before relating the events of that Thursday night, it is best to briefly tell about each of the Elders since each one had their own peculiarities.

First of all, there was George Moore. George served as the Field Overseer at the time and was having extreme family problems especially between him and his wife. Subsequently, he seemed always on the defensive and was often abrupt. The main trouble with George is he could not keep his mouth shut. Most of the time he would relate to others the gist of the private Elder's meetings as well as any personal matters of any of the membership. As you might imagine, his parts on the meetings often reflected this trait. Later on that year George was removed as an Elder for these very reasons.

Then there was William Boyd, a well-meaning man who served as the Bible Study Overseer. William had suffered from cancer but it was reported to be in remission. His wife was also not in good health and accordingly they were both limited in their efforts to serve. As a result, Brother Boyd felt inadequate and unqualified to serve as an Elder.

Bernard Berry was the Sunday service overseer, of which he was very happy about, since this position required very little effort. Although most of the congregation viewed Bernard as the friendliest of Elders, at the end he seemed least cooperative. I suppose the reason for this is that his wife had a very tight hold over him. She constantly objected to her husband's time being tied up with Elder matters, therefore making his availability limited.

The Theocratic School Overseer and probably the man I resented most at the time, was Art Stand. What can I say about Art? He will more than likely be late for his own funeral! Art was not dependable and yet viewed himself more knowledgeable and experienced than any of the other elders. It was very difficult to get Art to cooperate since following instructions was not one of his attributes. Art was to have a profound effect on me that Thursday night, a night I'll never forget. He too, was later removed as an Elder for reasons listed above.

Then there was the man I admired most for many years up to that night. I had virtually patterned my life after him and even once told him that someday I would occupy his position. That night I was occupying the position that he had for many years. However, I had noticed that during the past year Brother Irvin Wilks had been lingering at his responsibility. Many had commented about his starry eyed look, as though he were preoccupied with something, other than the meetings. Irvin had a great many responsibilities and his wife was at very low ebb. They rarely spoke to each other, at least decently and she was constantly finding fault with Irvin and the congregation.

I had always viewed Paul Rider as a man with the purest of hearts. I have always thought very highly of Paul and consider him the most loving of brothers. However, Paul had a very large family and was required to work long and hard hours, secularly, in order to provide for their necessities. It was often difficult for Paul to be dependable as far as being on time and fulfilling his duties.

Brother Steve Angle had not been with the congregation long but had been appointed an Elder although he held no position of responsibility except to conduct a book study on Tuesday nights.

Steve had one major problem. Insecurity! The Angle's had moved many times since I had first met them years earlier. In addition to this, he had changed jobs as often as he changed shirts. Subsequently, few people exercised confidence in him. However, he was a kind and loving brother, always willing to cooperate.

Brother Jim Core had been in the church for many years. During those years, Jim had been a presiding overseer in Norfolk, Virginia and was very knowledgeable. There was no question that the congregation respected Jim. However, at that time he had been displaying instability. Jim had agreed to quit his very stable job and go partners with Brother Charles Monday in the cabinet making business. The business had started failing and Jim and Charlie had started bickering and their spirituality was fast going down the drain. Prior to that Thursday in April of 1977 a committee met with these Brothers and the partnership ended abruptly with severe hard feelings. I couldn't believe what I had witnessed and there is no doubt in my mind that this increased my downward plunge to leaving the church.

As you can see, all these men had problems, which is nothing unusual. However these are not the normal problems that face a church. These are things that the Bible specifically has solutions for and they are readily accessible. The final results were preoccupied Elders, poor participation and poor efforts in preparation and in meeting attendance. All of these things are what congregations readily pick up on and soon start to complain about. As one might expect, God's spirit cannot remain where such a condition prevails.

There were many personalities that greatly influenced me either positively or adversely, that became the *Unforeseen Occurrence* that would affect me forever.

J. Lee Gilbert

Chapter 2

THE COST OF NEGATIVE THOUGHTS

By now I was entertaining negative thoughts about my associates also my responsibilities and even my family. Little things became big nightmares and it soon became apparent. Then came the final straw that will never be forgotten.

The ministry school was to start at 7:30 that Thursday night. As usual, the late arrivals strolled in nonchalantly disturbing the few dependable. There were two schools and I was the Ministry School Overseer. The first four students went on without a hitch however, about half way through the program, my son Kevin, became ill. While attending to him, one of the Elders came to inform me the last scheduled speaker had not arrived and was up next to speak. I rushed to the podium, my hands still wet in vomit from the clean up of my son, to fill in for a delinquent. Sadly, my young son was left alone in the bathroom while I had to take care of the congregation.

Needless to say, the sermon that followed was anything but pleasant! As I spoke you could hear a pin drop on the carpet. "Can you imagine Jesus Christ not showing up after he had made a commitment?" I ask, does not the very book we are preaching from state: "Do unto others as you would have them do unto you". (Matthew 7: 12.) Do these principles only apply to those on the outside?" I spoke for what seemed to be a lifetime but in reality was only six minutes. In essence, my sermon was clearly about my filling in for delinquents and that one's responsibility should be just that, responsible!

Upon my decent from the stage, I gathered my things and family and made my exit. Brother Berry, one of the Elders approached and tried to offer comfort and encouragement but frankly, it was to late. I had made up my mind this was the last time I would be in the church.

There were no words spoken during our trip home. Halfway there I stopped at a Seven Eleven store in Great Bridge, Chesapeake, Virginia to buy a six-pack of Michelob beer and still not a word. At home my wife and children prepared and went to bed while I sat in the middle of the living room floor, playing my guitar and drinking my first ever-alcoholic beverage. When morning arrived, I cleaned up and departed never to return home again. Of course, that proved to be a fatal mistake as I learned several years later.

That same day, I found a Sears department store and loaded up my car with every western wear accessory that was available, including a blue hard brim cowboy hat. For years I had dreamed of a "Home on the Range" and now planned to pursue that life free from the ministry. The poem I wrote years later called: "Continental Cowboy", reflects that very thought and in fact was inspired by those events. The poem appears in my book *Reflections In Poetry* on page sixty-seven.

Several months earlier, I had started going to a Steak & Eggs coffee shop for some personal time and to write my pest control proposals but it proved to be the first steps to a new kind of life. The waitress, Karen Martin, was a five foot two beautiful brunette that proved to be more than just a waitress. She was the beginning of my *Unforeseen Occurrence*, the first of a series of building blocks that helped mold my life, and events I would not trade for all the tea in China.

J. Lee Gilbert

Chapter 3

FOUR WHEEL DRIVE IS OVER

It was seven thirty on that Friday night and I was this green horn cowboy looking dude that walked into this red neck bar, having no clue what to expect next, but I was ready none the less. Ordering a beer and acting like I knew what I was doing. I sat at the bar until Karen Martin and the gang arrived.

Although she never said, it is my guess she knew I was not what I pretended. After all, my life began at high school and then straight into the ministry. There had been no time to experience the ways of the world. Therefore I walked, talked and looked like a city slicker although as a minister I regularly spoke about the follies of the world.

At the same time, Karen now had someone she could mold into her own. So the lesson began. It was my first but not my last drunken stupor. That night, Karen and I kept the little dance floor hot until about two o'clock in the morning, while the small crowd that was there watched us dance the night away. That night I truly learned what the world was all about and what I thought I had been missing.

After I had made serious love with Karen in the car outside the bar, I promised to be in touch. I parted and headed for my broken home. Arriving around three fifteen in the morning and smelling of beer and cigarettes I planted myself on the living room sofa and fell asleep still wearing my cowboy attire.

To my surprise, I slept until two o'clock in the evening undisturbed. My wife helped me up and prepared a good dinner without asking where I had been or what I had done. As for the kids it was life as normal. Needless to say, there were no more church meetings for me.

That weekend, the rhythm guitarist of my band and spiritual comrade telephoned to arrange band practice. However, there was an ulterior motive for his call, as I would soon learn.

Band practice was scheduled for two o'clock in the evening at my house and I was ready. When Bob Bates and Sam Moore arrived it was not to practice. They started questions about what I thought I was doing to my family. I ignored their efforts and started warming up. At that point they began to pack up their equipment virtually breaking up a successful band. This was another price paid to escape my old life style. I remember later driving to Richmond, Virginia and hearing a radio station announcing my band, "Four Wheel Drive" would be appearing at Lamplighter's Club in Norfolk, Virginia, that evening. It was not going to happen because Four Wheel Drive had broken up and did not exist!

Since my wife, and kids had gone to her mom's house, I packed up my clothes and guitar and moved out. Karen and I had arranged for an apartment in Norview a part of Norfolk, Virginia. This would prove to be a bad move but full of learning about the world and sowing my oats.

J. Lee Gilbert

Chapter 4

A NEW LIFE

When I arrived at the apartment it was only to find it cold and empty. In my haste to escape my former life, there was no time for planning. There was not any furniture not even a chair to sit in or a television to keep me company. In the kitchen were paper plates and plastic utensils, a frying pan and a few pots.

Karen and her daughter, Carri arrived shortly thereafter to begin our new life together. That night and for several weeks after, we slept on sheets spread across the living room floor. This was the perfect formula for a bad back and poor posture.

My first experience with diabetes was about to begin. The life depicted on television of would be studs, is far from the truth. You still have responsibilities such as a secular job, a home to care for and bills to pay. On our first full night together, I learned how to give Carri a diabetic shot. Karen had to be at work at six in the morning. So I had to make sure Carri got her shot and off to school.

It was not long after my new responsibilities were complete, I was sitting on a bar stool at the Steak and Eggs restaurant watching

Karen in her mini skirt waiting on tables. It never dawned on me at that point, what I had given up in exchange for this life. The old folks use to say! "What goes around comes around". A lesson I was about to learn in a brutal way.

By the time we returned home I discovered quickly we had nothing in common. Karen talked like a Sailor; smoked like it was going out of style and had a telephone transplanted to her ear in which she used it constantly. The results were I spent most of my early evenings with my guitar.

That proved to be a bad idea in that it gave me time to think of my children. Of course that brought me down and by the time we went to bed I was not in a love making frame of mind. Naturally, that was not the way to develop a successful relationship.

Often I was in that state of mind and it was apparent to Karen she had made a bad decision. To make matters worse, at my job I had been promoted to Branch Manager's position and would soon be transferred from Virginia Beach, Virginia to Richmond, Virginia. After the transfer, nightly, after work, I would drive home about 150 miles back to Norfolk, Virginia only to be depressed.

There were some bright moments and although at the time, I had no idea how important it would be later that I began writing. I guess as a release, a form of weeping and getting it all out of my system. One poem worthy of mentioning was called A Poem For

An Invalid. One afternoon, on the way back to my office, the thoughts crossed my mind and pulled off the interstate and I wrote this poem down in just a few minutes.

I mention this poem at this time because it was Karen's mom that fell in love with the poem. One Sunday, Karen came home with her Mom's church bulletin and my poem had appeared on the back page. We were surprised, proud and very happy. Soon, the happiness would dissipate and the first of many bad relationships would begin. I did not know it then, but that poem, years later would appear in one of my first books.

J. Lee Gilbert

Chapter 5

THE BIG MOVE

Daily, I went with Karen to the restaurant and by six thirty I was on my way to Richmond, Virginia to work. Karen was beginning a new relationship behind my back. Ironically, it was with a police officer and his name also was Lee. That affair lasted for months and during that time Karen was also developing a strong relationship with my estranged wife.

It became apparent I was loosing Karen, which made my wife happy, thinking her marriage might be saved anyway. The fact of the matter was that Karen and my estranged wife were almost successful in having a meeting with me together one Sunday afternoon.

I was to meet Karen at another Steak and Eggs restaurant and eagerly I arrived early thinking I was about to save my relationship with Karen. To my surprise, Dawn, my estranged wife and Karen had become good friends and plotted to save my marriage. However, Dawn arrived at the restaurant at the same time Karen did. I knew this scene was not going to happen and I made my exit. Both of them tried to catch me but I left in a fury. Suffice it to say, my relationship with Karen had ended and another life began.

Returning to the apartment, I began packing to move to Richmond, Virginia and to my job there. Not aware then, these events were slowly breaking me inside preparing me for a life threatening catastrophic event in the near future.

My office in Richmond, Virginia had been an old farmhouse almost out in nowhere land. When I first saw it I thought either I'm at the wrong address or the owner of my company made a very bad decision. I had been there a couple of weeks earlier with my immediate boss that explained that the owner knows what he is doing. That proved to be true because when I left the company later, this Richmond office was number four out of eighteen locations in the entire company.

My boss, John Parks, brought me up to meet all the employees. He took me to lunch and at the end of the evening he gave me a new brief case and a daily planner. That planner proved to be my first step to keeping a diary, as I have for almost thirty years to date. Most of the details found in this book were derived from those diaries.

Since my new office had been formally a private residence, I was able to live there in the evening and work there during the day. My evenings were long and lonely. Oh, yes, I had a nice car a special addition roadrunner! I had a vasectomy and was ready to find the right women, but nothing had yet brought me comfort nor kept me warm at night.

In the mornings things really brightened up. My secretary, Charlotte Hardy, would come in the office early and fix breakfast for us. At that point, I began to put on the pounds that would later add to my unforeseen circumstance. I made several weekly trips to and from Norfolk, Virginia to see my children. Each of those trips was about a hundred-mile drive. I was slowly ruining my health and future.

Of course, my newfound smoking habit added to my health problem not to mention the mess of ashes everywhere and cigarette burn holes in my clothes.

Then there was my effort to cover my newly found habit so my children would not find out but I did not realize the smell is impossible to cover. However, neither the children nor their mother ever said a word. They were just happy to see their dad! It proved to be another bad decision leading to that *Unforeseen Occurrence* in nineteen eighty-two.

J. Lee Gilbert

Chapter 6

FIRED!

Finally, my loneliness and strong desire to be with my children lead me to contact Dawn and I convinced her to see each other again. By this time, I had been removed from the church. As a result, when I started back to church with Dawn, I was treated like someone with a communicable disease. It really did not matter because by now I was getting used to the treatment. By winter, after a few months, we rented a large four-bedroom home. It was fully carpeted with a nice fireplace but our relationship was never the same. Frankly, during the night I would stare at the ceiling and think about Karen who by now was very happy with the policeman named Lee.

Then the pattern started again. During the day I made sales calls and would stay at a restaurant called Lum's and write my business letters and proposals for the pest control company I worked for. It was here, on the other side of the counter, I met a beautiful red head named Brenda. She was fully endowed wearing a mini skirt and smoking a cigarette. She proved to be my next affair victim. Although, somehow I knew I would "reap what I would sow"!

I had convinced Dawn to move to south Richmond and out of the huge three-story house into a more affordable three-bedroom two-bath ranch. It proved to be just what the doctor ordered, so to speak, for my future life with Brenda.

The strain on my marriage began for what proved to be the last. Each afternoon I was in the restaurant building a relationship with Brenda. As for the home front, Dawn and the kids soon were gone, this time leaving everything behind.

Later, Brenda and her two children moved in and it was perfect. Brenda would drive my special edition Road Runner to work and I had a company car. I thought I was on top of the world! Little did I know, soon part of my world would collapse.

Brenda and I became a hot item and we kept the streets and the bars hot! I spent most of my time at work at Brenda's job or out party bound, smoking and drinking my life and health away not realizing the effects of such a life. It would soon reflect on my job and it's successful performance.

One afternoon my boss, John Parks, had come to my office in Richmond as he had always done to check on the operation of the office. Since my office had been rated the number four branch out of the entire company, I was happy to see John and to boast a bit. It was my eighth anniversary and I just knew good things were on the way. Wrong!

That afternoon John came in my office and I immediately

started talking about my anniversary. This time he was very solemn, as he asked me to be seated. He explained the company prefers that their managers be family men and very stable. However that was not true of me and it appeared there was no chance of it ever happening. Therefore, effective immediately, I was fired!

It took about forty-five minutes for it to set in and what a blow. Of course I tried desperately to get John to explain, but to no avail. He did inform me of a nice severance package that included three months pay with insurance coverage.

Needless to say, I was devastated! I finally built up the nerve to call Brenda and broke the news and asked her to pick me up at the office.

Once again the pressure was on and it would show up in a devastating manner. I thought to myself people today have no clue how their life style, their temperament and even their thought patterns can adversely effect their health.

For several weeks I was so depressed and walked around acting as if my world and life had ended. Soon I would discover in my mind anyway, everything happens for a reason. In fact, it proved to be a blessing in disguise. In the future, because of my new business venture, I would learn the value of expansion and diversification. These qualities proved to be priceless during my trip through my *Unforeseen Occurrences.*

J. Lee Gilbert

Chapter 7

STARTING ALL OVER AGAIN

My day of reckoning with life finally came around. By that time I was so involved with Brenda I did not care about the divorce and what it entailed. The finale proved disastrous for me but not until years later. Another *Unforeseen Occurrence* that would last nine and a half years. Almost like being in prison.

In the attorney's office that morning, I was eager to sign the divorce papers and leave. Although we covered the details, they did not sink in due to my desire to leave the attorney's office. The end result was I signed everything over to my soon to be ex-wife. Months later it dawned on me how foolish I had been but now with no recourse. In essence, I agreed to pay eight hundred dollars a month in support. She also got everything, the furniture and car plus I had to pay health coverage. What did I get? I got a new sports car and her permission to get a vasectomy. Somehow I knew after marrying Dawn when I was only seventeen years old and having two children I did not want to have any more kids. Needless to say, in retrospect, "she got the gold mine and I got the shaft". At that point I did not care because I just wanted out!

Besides I thought I had no intentions of living up to the deal of paying this ungodly amount of support in which Dawn did not really need, after all her family was very well off. I did not realize unforeseen occurrences befall us all and my decision would haunt me through the majority of the upcoming years.

By this time I had become very good friends with Brenda's bosses, Frank and Zol Mitchell. They owned all the Lum's restaurants in Richmond, Virginia. They asked me to join them in the ownership; one that lasted years after Brenda was gone. Shortly after my divorce was final I developed two new replacements: an intense relationship with Brenda, alcohol and a strong partnership with Frank and Zol. At nights and weekends, Brenda and I would party the night away. The rest of my time was spent working either in entomology, the study of insects or with the restaurants. This schedule was so intense and would prove later an important role in the events of 1982. The aftermath was no time for my children who were the real victims.

Almost immediately after the divorce was final, Brenda and I planned a vacation to Fort Lauderdale, Florida. Her ex- husband lived there because he was avoiding his child support. Few states had child support laws and Florida was one that didn't enforce the payment of child support. So, every summer Brenda would send her kids to stay with her ex-husband since he offered no assistance. Another deadbeat dad!

For the first time in her life, thanks to me, she had a means to make the trip and have a vacation of a lifetime all at the expense of my children. By now, my children were cooped up at their grandparents home living a very strict religious life that would effect them for the rest of their lives, a fact, I believe, that has led to their current life style. I'm reminded of a song called: "Cats In A Cradle", perfect description of my life.

After dropping off Kate and Bunk, Brenda's kids, we spent two weeks on the Miami beaches. Then we packed up and left for Tennessee to visit Graceland and I was in heaven! It was at the time when Elvis' Uncle was in the hospital. The first morning we were at Graceland at 7 a.m. at the front gate when a truck drove up to exit and it was Elvis' uncle! He stopped to talk with us a while and allowed us to take pictures. I was elated! It was shortly afterward; we heard the news about Elvis' passing. In fact, I still have tickets to a show we were planning to attend but the king died first so I kept the tickets in memory.

The final leg of our journey was to the Grand Old Opery and all our country music idols. By this time, Brenda was into Conway Twiddy and I loved Hank Williams Jr. and all the outlaws. It would reflect in my writing many years later. It was obvious too in my dress that I was cowboy all the way! Years later, I would write a poem called Continental Cowboy that appeared in the book *Reflections In Poetry* and reflected well my life style of the eighties and nineties. That book went on to be nominated for the Pulitzer Prize, along ways from the *Unforeseen Occurrence* of nineteen eighty-two.

Chapter 8

THE PRESSURE BEGINS

By now my severance pay was coming to an end and I needed to locate a new job. The restaurant income was nice but was not what I wanted to do with my life. Then there was my child support and the fulfillment of the contract I foolishly signed earlier.

As luck would have it, one day out of the blue, I got a phone call from Bert Dodson, Sr., owner of Dodson Brothers Pest Control of Lynchburg, Virginia who offered me a job I could not refuse. The position was a Regional Manager's job to oversee his Carolina region, which would include North and South Carolina, and Tennessee. The money was perfect along with the benefits package. I had always considered Burt Dodson Sr. as truly a southern gentleman, soft-spoken man that walked softly and yet carried a big stick, so to speak. However, there was one problem and that was what to do with Brenda?

To my surprise, she was very receptive to the idea of moving to Charlotte, North Carolina when the school year was over. For several months, I drove to my office in North Carolina and spent each week traveling to each of my offices.

Upon my acceptance of the position, there were three regions. Of course, my region was in last place in the company and had been for years. I needed to act fast to make a change and so called an old friend in Richmond, Bill Working and the President of Commonwealth Realty. Bill had several properties in North Carolina and of course he contracted with me and almost immediately my region moved to number one and I was riding high! The moral of that story is, it's not what you know but it's whom you know!

By this time Brenda and the kids were packed up and ready to go. The company was paying all the expenses including a brand new company car with leather seats. We were going in style! The Mitchell Corporation gave us a going away party and now we were set.

However, not everything was peaches and cream. On the day the movers were to pack us up, it snowed leaving eighteen inches of the white stuff on the ground. We were stranded for four days in a motel and were stir crazy by the time we left for Charlotte, North Carolina.

It had not snowed there and setting up house was a breeze but life there was anything but! Brenda and the kids became isolated and I was their only contact with the world, a no win situation to say the least.

The strain began to show and soon in several forms. When the kids enrolled in school, they were months behind because the North Carolina schools were so advanced and even more strict. I was always on the road, which left Brenda alone, and finally, the move separated us from our families.

There were some bright moments though few and far between. Because of my previous experience with carpenter ants, Ed Pinigus, the technical director for the company, ask that I give a one day class on proper carpenter ant treatment of a home. Enrolling Brenda's help, together we spent two weeks constructing a model house that I could use to demonstrate treatment techniques. The school was perfect and I was flying high!

Then there was my negative experience with Ed Pinigus. One day he asked me to come to his office and upon entering he asked was I familiar with the term: frugal? He handed me a dictionary and ask me to look it up. "Read and heed!" he instructed. The end results were a strained relationship with the second in command. No one likes to be talked down to and it never produced anything positive. Years later in the book; *You Can't Judge A Book By It's Cover*, on page 82 I wrote: Three Things I Hate, which was inspired by that experience. Needless to say, I did not like being talked down to.

Soon things began to fall apart and I would be out the door! The straw that broke the camel's back was getting my paycheck.

Usually, it was sent to the Richmond office and even once sent to Anne Jackson at the Norfolk branch. Finally, in frustration, I called Burt Dodson Sr. and explained I needed my pay on time like everyone else and one more late check and I would be history! Of course, Mr. Dodson was a true gentleman and assured me the problem would be resolved.

In spite of his good intentions, on the very next pay day there was no check and I was out the door. I telephoned Brenda and ask her to start packing. Then I arranged to pick up a U-Haul truck and we were set to move.

There were two steps in order to have a smooth transition; we needed a place to live and I needed a job. Again, I called on my contacts and customers for help.

First, I telephoned Chateau Village apartments, another Bill Working property and arranged for an apartment and they even had the electricity connected so we were set when we arrived.

Finally, I telephoned an old friend at Parliament Pest Control to arrange a job. The owner, Ray News, told his manager, Joe Lupini, to hire me and let me do anything until he arrived that next Tuesday.

So, with my personal car hooked to the back of the U-Haul and with Brenda and the kids in my company car, we arrived back in Richmond, Virginia around two a.m. that morning and exhausted. That morning we slept on the floor and planned to unpack on

Sunday. It might have appeared like everything was rosy but it was only a façade because unknowingly my hourglass was fast running out of sand.

J. Lee Gilbert

Chapter 9

THE SECOND HEART BREAK

Brenda was able to return to her old job at Lum's restaurant and even I began to work there part time. I did not know it at the time but that job would play an important role in the rest of my life and the *Unforeseen Occurrence* that befalls us all.

That same week I would meet with Ray News and Joe Lupini to solidify my employment. From the very start I had the best relationship with my immediate boss, Joe Lupini. He too, would play a major part in the rest of my life even up to today.

There were four other individuals that proved to be key players and they also were employees at Parliament Pest Control Company. The first was David Anderson, Joe Lupini's nephew. Also, there was Billy Hawks, who was one of those good old boys. Tim Howell, a habitual liar but he proved to have a heart of gold. Finally, there was Lemuel Kidd, a black man that everyone loved and he is missed by all of us today.

Before long, I was on top of the world again. Sales for me at Parliament Pest Control were unbelievable but due to my chosen path I was always broke. After all, the most important thing to me, were not my children, instead it was Brenda and partying on the town, a typical deadbeat dad. Needless to say, it led me to the *Unforeseen Occurrence.*

Although it was not evident to me, Brenda was already developing wondering eyes. She seemed so supportive but it was with an ulterior motive in mind. She encouraged me to work both jobs day and most nights, which freed her to roam the town while she left her children unattended. Like a fool, I trusted her to be at home performing her parental responsibility. I was so wrong!

One thing I learned as a Minister and Missionary; "Whatever a man is sowing this he shall also reap". (Gal.6: 7,8) and that was true of Brenda too. One night, while working at Lum's, a friend of Brenda's telephoned and asked if I could stop at the Ramada Inn before I went home and deliver a message to someone. In reality, the friend knew Brenda was there with another man and wanted me to see it for myself.

What a horrible experience! I pulled up to the motel and just at the entrance were Brenda and this man, they were doing some serious kissing with each other in the parking lot! I pulled up beside them and watched for what seemed like forever before she finally turned to look my way. She looked as though she had seen a ghost. She returned inside the motel in a hurry as I left squealing tires and filling the air with smoke from my speedy escape.

Of course, within a couple of hours I was drunk and prepared for retribution. I returned to the motel and the car I had bought for Brenda was still there. Vengefully, I almost destroyed her car on the inside. I ripped out all the wiring in the dashboard and made a mess of the inside. Finally, I deflated all four tires and thought she could use the motel as her new home!

By the time the police arrived, I was already home crying in my beer. Although I did nothing wrong except destroy my own car, the officer stayed with me awhile to ensure my safety. During his visit he said, "I can't offer you a drink because you're already drunk." "Do you smoke?" He offered me my first cigarette. A habit that would also help lead me to that *Unforeseen Occurrence* on September 19th 1982, a day I'll never forget. From that night forward, smoking became a regular part of my life as my downward spiral began to intensify.

J. Lee Gilbert

Chapter 10

THE GOOD OLE' BOYS

Not long after my separation from Brenda, two of my friends and workmates moved into my home. This proved to be a major highlight in my life. They were David Anderson and Billy Hawks. In time, we became known as the " Good Old Boys" and we sure knew how to party and did so every Thursday, Friday and Saturday night.

Brenda moved back in after a few weeks because she and the kids had no place to go. She promised to find an apartment and would leave as soon as possible but she stayed for months instead of a couple of weeks.

It appeared to me that she was not making an effort to leave at all so I began to pull some strings myself. An old friend of mine, Claude Brookes with Mountain Property Management ran an apartment complex called Country Road Apartments. Some of the apartment units were government controlled and based on your income. I was able to secure one for Brenda with a real sob story and introduced her as my sister. The Good Old Boys moved her in and my life with Brenda was over for good! All she left me was a couple of bad habits, cigarette smoking and alcohol. Suffice it to say, this contributed to that upcoming event in my life that would change me forever. Like the fool I had become and in spite of all Brenda had done to me, still I was willing and did buy her a house warming gift, a coffee maker, what a foolish man I had become to stand there with my cheeks pulled apart for Brenda to ram me with a ten foot pole while my kids went lacking.

I continued my job at Lum's restaurant that led to a lot of hot dates. In fact, I started keeping a record in my company appointment book that soon developed into a diary, which to this day has provided me with a valuable source of information for this book.

Generally, on Friday night, the guys and myself were home by three in the afternoon and each of us had a responsibility toward the cause. Billy would pick up the Vodka, David got the Jim Beam and I would clean up the car. By six o'clock in the evening we were flipping a coin for the bathroom, the music was blasting and by nine o'clock p.m. we were three sheets in the wind! By the time we made it to the car we were beyond the legal drinking limit to drive but we were more interested in having fun.

Our main hang out was this cozy little bar in Ashland, Virginia called J.P.'s. There was a hot band there, specializing in southern rock and country music that was just our cup of tea. In fact, in time I became friends with a band member and I would fill in for him and play guitar from time to time.

One Friday night we arrived early and were ready to party. About eight-thirty that evening, three ladies walked in and right away we began to pick our babe for the night. David fell in lust with Jackie, a beautiful red head that David nicknamed "Jackie by Crackie". Billy decided in favor of Madeline and as for me it was Bonnie.

Later I learned not to *Judge A Book By It's Cover*, the title of my second book. You would never know by looking at Bonnie that she was so plagued with problems. On the outside she would have put Madonna to shame. What you did not see was a woman with three rebellious children that lived in a section eight or low-income property. She had a boyfriend named Hunter that was half her age and an ex-husband named Bailey that lived in Florida in order to dodge his child support obligations. Another deadbeat dad!

That night though we only had one thing in mind! Billy and David landed on both feet and were rounding second base. I approached Bonnie but she told me about Hunter and was only there to listen to the band. I was sitting at our table dejected when Billy and David returned. We had made a bet about getting those girls on the dance floor and they knew I would be paying the bill. Instead, they went to Bonnie and began to raise hell with her for rejecting me.

Soon they were back on the dance floor and as for me, I sent a drink over to Bonnie with an apology note excusing my friends. To my surprise, she came over to my table to talk and before long we were on the dance floor all night long. In fact, I drove her home and we sat in my car until 4 a.m. needless to say, although I won the bet, as you will see, it cost me dearly. In fact, my second book entitled; *You Can't Judge A Book By It's Cover* was written and inspired by such like people that have passed through my life. Most of them had two faces, one with a frown covered by a smile as mentioned in my third book, *Reflections In Poetry*, in the poem called Plastic Smile On A Plastic Face.

Chapter 11

BACK ON TRACK! THE THIRD TRY

At this point my life was back on track. At work the sales were skyrocketing and due to my sales the company was growing fast. It had always been the desire of the owner of Parliament, Ray News, to open an office in Virginia Beach, Virginia and since I was born and raised in Tidewater, I was his choice to be the Regional Manager there.

That was good news for me but it presented some serious challenges. Bonnie had three children and each one was in school. As for her middle child, Jim, he was nothing but trouble. Many times we found ourselves out at 2 a.m. trying to find an under aged delinquent. On several occasions we found him passed out lying in a ditch somewhere in the neighborhood.

One morning when we arrived home from J.P.'s, we discovered Jim was nowhere to be found. We rode and walked everywhere in search of Jim. Finally, in desperation, we called the police. Since Jim was a juvenile and under age the trouble he might get into would lead to real problems for his mom and me.

As fate would have it, the police found him passed out in a

ditch a couple miles from the house. It goes without saying, I was very upset and it became very evident. After the smoke had cleared, it was time for a confrontation! I was wrong to let my temper and emotions take control. The truth is if we had been responsible parents instead of being at J. P.'s, we should have been at home looking after the kids.

At any rate, I started on Jim and before long our shouting match became a fistfight! Of course, I had the upper hand, after all, I was older and he was very drunk. Needless to say, I beat the hell out of him and it took Bonnie to pull me off of him at which point he was gone again. Looking back, I realize how wrong I was and why hindsight is always twenty-twenty.

Again the police had to find Jim and brought him back to the house. That morning the police told Jim he was lucky "Mr. Gilbert did not break both hands on you". That's right, that morning I broke my left hand on his hard head. Sad!

Bonnie and I ended up in the emergency room where I met and later became good friends with Doctor Steve Lanett. It was my first but not my last encounter with Steve. After a week or so when the swelling went down, I received and wore my first cast for about eight weeks. It was the first time too for me to learn how to write with my right hand. An experience that would prove to be valuable later because my *Unforeseen Occurrence* in nineteen eighty-two left me without the use of my left hand. That was just the beginning. That episode put pressure on Bonnie to ask the authorities for help. Before long, Jim was in court and the Judge gave him some serious responsibilities that Jim literally hated. My favorite was washing police cars! Also, he was ordered to build a model for a science project and he had to attend cap classes along with his parents. In other words, again, I was paying for another individual's wrong. This proved to be more pressure that led me to the *Unforeseen Occurrence* of September 1982.

J. Lee Gilbert

Chapter 12

THE TRANSFER

For months, Joe Lupini and I went to Virginia Beach trying to find a building to establish an office. At the same time I was to start planting seeds in an effort to develop new business. As new accounts were secured, then I began running the new route until a technician was hired and trained.

As if that were not enough, I also began my search for a new home. That was tricky because there was only one income and five mouths to feed. What a fool I was to think this new life I was in now was better than the career I left behind when I was a minister. I had been blinded by hatred and a desire to establish my own life free from the influence of God. What a fool!

After almost a year, Joe and I found a nice building on the corner of Witchduck Road and Virginia Beach Boulevard in Virginia Beach and Ray News, the owner, came down to buy the building and then we were off and running. I was not aware then of the roadblocks that were just ahead.

I had an old friend from my Dodson days named Leon Flinn and he was my first service technician. Earlier we had hired Donna

Swain to be the receptionist although at first she filled every position from painter to housekeeper and never complained. We started out with a great team but it too was riddled with problems.

First of all there was Leon. I was not aware of his problem with alcohol. At Dodson Termite and Pest Control he had been the perfect manager but since those days the bottle had taken over his life. I wasn't sure which would kill him first, his smoking or the alcohol.

As for me, well, I was slowly becoming a nervous wreck. I was having trouble at home with Bonnie because of her kids and we needed to move and had no money. To make matters worse, like a fool, I refused to let her move to Virginia Beach without the benefit of a marriage license. So, she agreed and now I was planning a new job; a move; a new house; another marriage and a new child support fight. The *Unforeseen Occurrence* was fast approaching!

We arranged a simple wedding that was quaint and included some of my friends and of course all of her family.

As fate would have it, on the day of the wedding, February fourteenth, it was snowing. However, the church was full and the wedding went on without a problem. To prove my vanity, the bride walked down the isle to "The Wedding Song" played by me via a recording. After a short ceremony and pictures, we went to the reception, which was held at her Aunt's house.

The Unforeseen Occurrence

After the smoke cleared, Bonnie and I were off to a local Holiday Inn for the honeymoon, which was less than blissful because it was that time of the month. Some friends had champagne on ice waiting in our room so we drank and watched T.V. another prelude of things to come.

J. Lee Gilbert

Chapter 13

SLIDING DEEPER DOWN HILL

Even as the number of this chapter indicates, the luck of the draw was not going my way. Bonnie stayed in Richmond and I moved to Virginia Beach securing a home in Lynnhaven. I spent almost all summer painting and preparing the house for Bonnie's arrival. Occasionally, I would bring a truckload from Richmond so that on the actual relocation, it would be quite simple.

The move was actually finished in July and from the start we had problems. In fact, that summer the temperature averaged ninety five to one hundred degrees and of course we only had two small window units for air conditioning. The humiture usually ran around one hundred ten plus! That kept us all on edge and made for some tense moments.

Often we were able to relieve the stress by frequent trips to the oceanfront, which was only three miles from the house. However, in July it was always bumper-to-bumper traffic and it took almost an hour and half to get to the beach. However, it was wonderful and we spent many nights strolling up and down the beach.

One highlight of our stay there that summer occurred along the

Atlantic Avenue beach line. While walking along the beach, we heard a faint voice in the distance calling, "Hey Mr. Gilbert"… and almost a hundred yards or more away was young Nick Lupini and some friends waving trying to get my attention. That impressed me because my experience with young people indicated they normally avoided adults especially when with their friends. To this day, Nick does not remember the moment although he grins from ear to ear when he hears me tell the story to others.

The pressure began to intensify in August that year and it came from several fronts. It came from the owner of the company, Ray News, because income was not as strong as he had hoped. My income was not near enough to support five people much less pay the $800.00 a month in child support. I began to put pressure on Bonnie to find a job, which really put our relationship in file thirteen.

The final pressure came from the state in the form of A.D. C. support issues. A representative from the state had contacted me, Mr. Ray, regarding my delinquency and was putting pressure on me to catch up. By this time, my smoking and drinking had reached new heights and it began to show in my appearance, weight and disposition.

As if that were not enough, Ray News came down with an ultimatum and that was sell or loose the office. At this point that notion had a good sound to it! On the home front, Bonnie was crying to go back home to Richmond and Joe Gallager, the Vice President, Joe Lupini, the Regional Director and even Ray News made it clear my old job was now in jeopardy.

The pressure was really mounting and I finally ask to be transferred back to the Richmond branch, my original office and my old position. It was a deal I could not pass up and so accepted it with open arms.

As for Bonnie, she had already given up her job and had already packed up and back in Richmond before you could say, jack rabbit and with a smile from ear to ear! As you might imagine, the pressure was reaching the boiling point and needed just one more event to cause the *Unforeseen Occurrence* that would change my life forever. So now I was sliding down hill at a high rate of speed heading for a crash landing!

J. Lee Gilbert

Chapter 14

THE NIGHTMARE BEGINS

The final straw that broke the camel's back was about to occur. Since I was transferring back to my old position so too my pay scale. There was not enough money to care for my obligations as a Regional Manager so understandably it would be disastrous on a salesman's pay.

In a last ditch effort, I telephoned my ex-wife, Dawn and explained my dilemma and ask if I could reduce my child support obligation from eight hundred to four hundred dollars a month and to my surprise she agreed and I was very happy to say the least!

Although broke as a yard bird, so to speak, I hired an attorney to write up a new agreement that I thought Dawn would accept even as she had acknowledged. Needless to say, I was dipping deep into our need for money but I figured the reduction would soon make up the difference.

After the necessary papers were completed, I met with the attorney so he could explain the details. He too had spoken to Dawn and everything seemed to be setting on go but my moment of truth was about to occur. My life would never be the same.

I remember the forty-five minute drive from my office to Hickory, Virginia where she was now living with her mother. During the drive I reflected on my childhood days when most of the area was woods with narrow winding roads with only two lanes, one going and one leaving. I remembered having to hitch hike from Great Bridge High School football practice every night on my way home usually getting a ride with my cousin or a neighbor. I remembered too traveling the same road during my ministry days in an effort to carry out some spiritual responsibility. Yet now I was embarking on a journey to sever my ties forever with that life. At least that is what I thought at that time.

It was early, September nineteenth and I arrived around 9:30 a.m. that morning at Dawn's. She answered the door with a smile and bad news! After thumbing through the legal documents I arranged, I had explained them in detail earlier via the phone, she calmly expressed a change of heart and refused to sign them. Of course, I wanted an explanation but none was offered. Belligerently, I explained the high cost of the attorney and my actions were based on her prior agreement but she displayed no concern. At this point I went ballistic and stormed away in a rage!

All the way back to my office, I was filled with hatred and reviewed every detail of my life leading up to this point. Had I made a bad decision and is there a way I could undo everything I had done? That was not my heart's desire but I did know one thing,

I learned in the ministry, "whatever a person is sowing, this he will also reap!" (Galatians 6: 7,8) I was about to learn that lesson first hand.

I arrived back at my office in a rage and told my secretary, I did not want to be disturbed. She could see I was upset and dared not question me about what was wrong. I closed my office door and prepared to type a letter to Mr. Ray, with the support enforcement authorities, asking that he could take whatever action he chose because I had given up.

I had written the letter by hand and had started typing it and about to start the second paragraph when I began to fill a little queasy and broke into a cold sweat. Feeling very strange, I went up to the front office to ask my secretary for an aspirin. She looked at me and I remember her expression and it was one of fear! She struggled through her purse but it was too late! I told her I must have lockjaw because I was unable to turn my head. In an instant I fell on the floor and began convulsing. From that moment on my life would never be the same! My moment of the *Unforeseen Occurrence* had just occurred.

J. Lee Gilbert

Chapter 15

SEPTEMBER TWENTIETH NINETEEN EIGHTY-TWO

It was September twentieth nineteen eighty-two. I was only thirty-two years old and for most people, not even halfway through my life. However, soon I would learn a lesson, in retrospect, I wish everyone could experience because it will change your life for the best.

Of course, I became unconscious, in a comma and for months I was not aware of what was happening to me. I was taken to Bayside Hospital and fortunately for me, it was merely minutes away from my office. As the ambulance rushed me to the hospital, Donna was on the phone to my immediate boss, Joe Lupini, who in turn contacted the owner, Ray News.

At the hospital and while on the way, I was in a constant state of convulsions and the rescue personnel did their best to keep me from suffocating on my own discharge. I was rushed straight to the emergency room where the doctors and staff did everything possible to stabilize me and to determine what was wrong and what had happened.

In the mean time, company employees scrambled to notify my

family and rounding them up was no easy task. However, within hours my wife, Bonnie, my ex-wife, Dawn and my Mom had been notified and were on their way.

By the time Bonnie arrived, my condition had been accessed and the prognosis was very bleak, to say the least! They explained to my family that I had had a cerebral hemorrhage and one of my vessels was leaking blood into my brain. It had been determined by the presents of blood in my spinal fluid. My family was told not to expect much because my chances of survival did not exist. In fact, in nineteen eighty-two, no left handed people ever survived a brain hemorrhage. Basically, the doctors were preparing my family for a funeral.

I should explain that the human body is very complex, to say the least, however there are many constants regarding it's operation. One of those constants is if a person is left handed; he is motivated from the right side of his brain. That is true in reverse for the right-handed person. The medical professionals had perfected the procedures on the right-handed population since, statistically, the majority of people in the world are right handed.

To illustrate my point, if you are left handed how hard is it to find a left handed guitar or a left handed baseball glove and ask yourself how hard it is to pitch left handed or to pitch to a left handed hitter? So too the problem is only intensified for the medical profession.

By the time my family was allowed to see me, I was wired up like a Christmas tree. Only the immediate family was allowed in and only for a few minutes each. Kevin, Beckie and their mom finally made it to the hospital and it was not a pleasant sight. The children were very upset because it was obvious the prognosis was not very good.

Ironic as it may sound, basically, I missed the whole thing. I felt no pain and had no clue what was taking place. As far as I was concerned, I was in a deep sleep. It would be months before I would be conscience and even many more before I became coherent.

To my family and friends, the hours turned into days; the days turned into weeks and the weeks turned into months. Although the doctors prepared my family for my passing somehow and for some reason, my body and spirit just would not give up! Years later I would be heard joking, "I was not good enough for heaven and I could not be trusted in hell so they left me here until they decided what to do with me".

Regularly, my spinal fluid was checked to see if the brain continued to bleed, with no change. As for Bonnie, she stayed in my room and eventually even her mother, Cleo, joined her. The strain was obvious.

After fourteen days, this hospital made it clear there was nothing more they could do. They encouraged my family to consider a nursing home for my final days. Since Bonnie was unable to commute from Richmond to Virginia Beach daily and not willing to give up on me yet, she requested I be transferred to The Medical College of Virginia in Richmond, Virginia.

The doctors made it clear to my family; I was not up to the trip and probably would not live through the transfer. However, Bonnie explained, "you don't expect him to live anyway, at least he will die trying!" Good for her! That was good for me, because due to that decision, I would survive.

I knew that because the night before my scheduled departure, an old friend named Jerri, came to see me before I left. I remember her shouting at me to get a response from me and she had to be restrained but during the shuffle I actually became conscience and knew what was happening although the doctors, my family and friends had no clue. Just like September nineteenth nineteen eighty-two was that *Unforeseen Occurrence*, there would be even more to follow.

There was many times during the ordeal that I knew what was going on around me but was unable to let anyone know. For instance, the ride from Virginia Beach to Richmond was bumpy and I felt very cold but was unable to communicate my feelings.

When we arrived at the Medical Collage of Virginia, employees made enough noise to wake up the dead but nobody knew it but me.

Chapter 16

MY HERO ARRIVES

Reluctantly, the doctors prepared for my departure, still unconscious and in a coma, tenderly, I was placed in an ambulance and by eleven o'clock we were on the way to The Medical College of Virginia in Richmond.

Bonnie made arrangements with my co-workers to move all our belongings back to Richmond and to put it in storage. She had a struggle with the landlord but he had no choice, after all, my destiny seemed obvious. When it was all said and done, my property had been scattered all over creation and years after my recovery, I was still collecting it back together. Bonnie moved in with her sister, Carolyn, along with the three kids and her mother.

To everyone's amazement I made the two-hour trip without a problem. At The Medical College of Virginia the doctors assigned to my case were, Dr. Michael Rosner, a neurologist, Dr. Sing, a world-renowned surgeon and Dr. John Harbison a neurologist, specializing in vision. Upon my arrival, the doctors ordered immediate blood transfusions to ensure a fresh supply to the brain, which in turn bought more time for analysis.

No one though anticipated the next trauma that I suffered a stroke! I progressed from bad to worse as the doctors frantically tried to stabilize me and set up my treatment program and to admit me into intensive care that became my home for longer than I care to remember.

The dilemma became clear; left-handed people never survived a cerebral Hemorrhage long enough to have developed a treatment procedure and so techniques had not been developed yet. Of course the stroke simply complicated the situation.

The doctors explained my situation to Bonnie and my family and after I became conscience, many months later, they in turn explained it to me. The only thing that spared me was the fact it bled to the outside of my brain and not inward. To bleed inside would have meant certain death.

I remember years later, while working at a Crown gas station in Richmond, my second full time job for nine and a half years, often thinking and wondering why and how blessed I had been. During my years in the ministry, I remembered too about "God's undeserved kindness" (James 4:6) and how true it was in my case.

Every so often a spinal tap was performed to measure my blood loss as it came from my brain. In time the bleeding stopped, which was miraculous and now came the moment of truth. The neurosurgical team assembled and a game plan developed to correct my problem.

Since I was left handed, the team had to be prepared to do what they were trained to do backwards. In the mean time, there were four operational procedures from the groin area in preparation for the main event. To this day, I refer to them as operations, for all I know that is what they were.

Finally, my spinal taps showed the bleeding had stopped. The doctors had explained to my family, the longer I lived, the longer my chances were of survival. Plans were completed for my surgery and the operating room prepared. My family and friends joined together in the waiting room for what proved to be an all day ordeal and anxious anticipation only expecting the worse.

At days end, Doctor Rosner and Dr. Sing came in the waiting room with unbelievable news of a successful operation! They explained, I had a long up hill battle and I was not out of the woods yet.

Although it appeared bleak, apparently my inner spirit and will power would not give up. The doctors were regularly amazed at my progress, which occurred while I was unconscious.

At one point during the ordeal, Dr. Rosner had written an article if you would, for the New England Journal of Medicine and American Medical Journal regarding my case and often during my stay in the Medical College of Virginia students of medicine would flow through my room to meet the Miracle Man.

Like the biblical character, Job, I had reached the bottom rung and only one direction I could go and that was up. There were more *Unforeseen Occurrence* yet left to occur.

Chapter 17

WHATEVER A MAN IS SOWING

I was placed in intensive care for what seemed to be a lifetime for my family but as for me, I missed the entire ordeal. No pain and not conscience I may as well have been dead and a far as I knew, that was the case.

During my stay in the I.C.U. it was a matter of constant yelling to get a reaction from me. "What is your name?" "How old are you?" "What year is it?" "Where are you?" "Are you going to sleep your life away?" "Do you have any children?" The list of questions was endless and they were at it three times a day.

There was never any rest for me it seemed. When in reality, I was never conscience. If the doctors were not drilling me there were nurses massaging me to improve my blood circulation. When the staff could not perform their duties, then Bonnie, her mom or her sister were busy at my side. Also every night there were close friends and co-workers always there. However, as time passed those friends soon disappeared. In short order, I was forgotten except for my old friends Ron and Sandra Ray. They brought me Seven Eleven coffee every night!

In fact, even after I left the hospital Ron and Sandra continued to visit me at my home. Ron was very good working with his hands in woodcrafts and subsequently made several plaques that were one of a kind just for me. Of course, as is normal for the gender, Bonnie developed an attitude toward them and soon they disappeared too.

Then, after a few weeks, the questions continued from the medical staff until one afternoon, when I ask my family, out of the blue, to write down the answers to those questions so I could respond and they would leave me alone. My response brought a cheer to the room from everyone present. The doctors expressed extreme relief and at the same time cautioned and emphasized to keep me calm at all times.

My head looked as if I were wearing a football helmet and it was very tight fitting to say the least. At least now I was stable and they prepared to move me to what proved to be my new home for a very long time.

The spinal taps continued and my diet mainly consisted of Tylenol with codeine. In turn, I slept most of the time not aware of my surroundings. Soon though, I became conscience, although disoriented to say the least. Upon learning of my fate, the depression set in and for the most part I cried all the time. I saw no hope for the future and was drowning in self-pity.

The doctors on the other hand were jubilant, not to mention my daily medical staff. All of them witnessed a miracle, to say the least, and felt proud to have been a part of the process.

The time came to remove my helmet and the room was full of excitement. To me, it was horrifying not knowing what to expect. I had suffered the brain hemorrhage; it was followed by a stroke and now my final calamity, blindness! The *Unforeseen Occurrence* continued.

The news of my blindness came as no shock to the doctors. They had already prepared my family of the possibility and in fact had encouraged them to apply for social security. My boss, Joe Lupini, had already gotten the ball rolling on my company insurance disability program. Thank God because by the time I got my first check, we were next to starving.

To be blind, to me, was a fate worse than death! First a brain hemorrhage, then the stroke and finally loosing my vision. I learned first hand the truth of "whatever a man is sowing this he shall also reap"! (Gal. 6: 7,8)

The time finally came for me to leave the hospital with a full regiment rehabilitation therapy scheduled. I had been so long on the catheter that when it was removed it was discovered my body function had stopped and needed a jump-start, so to speak. At any rate, I was finally released and scared to death not knowing what the next *Unforeseen Occurrence* would be.

I did know my future looked very bleak. I had been in the

hospital for what seemed like forever and endured five operations, dozens of spinal taps, a stroke and now blindness. I had lost two homes and my job because I was no longer able to work and my future seemed to depend on a meager insurance check of nine hundred forty nine dollars and twenty-three cents. However, my will to return to normalcy was strong and my will power inside would not take no for an answer. To illustrate the severity of my condition below is a reprint of a letter from Dr. Michael Rosner to Dr. John Harbison from February 17, 1983.

Dear John:

I saw J. Lee Gilbert at the microsurgical clinic now about four to five months after subarachnoid hemorrhage and placement of a v-p shunt. His complaints remain relatively static. He has occasional mild headaches and a feeling of fullness at the top of the head. He complains of markedly decreased memory particularly long-term memory. His alexia is improving particularly if he is able to read the letters and assemble them into a known word. His left hemianopia remains static.

Because of my impending departure and his problems I have asked that you see him again for a follow-up of his deficits and particularly his potential for prisms. I feel that this will be a big help to J. Lee. His shunt at the moment seems to be working well and his fundi are normal; as you remember he had gross papilledema before his v.p shunt. Thanking you in advance for caring for this gentleman, I remain,

Sincerely yours,

Michael J. Rosner, M.D., F.A.C.S.

Recently, I contacted Dr. Rosner for an explanation of my shunt and it's purpose for me. His response is as follows:

Hi J. Lee,

A shunt (in your case) provides an alternate path for spinal fluid to be removed from the inside of the brain. Spinal fluid is produced at a constant rate in both the healthy and those with damaged brains but it must be absorbed at the same rate and low pressure or it will cause damage due to excess pressure. Some strokes (yours) associated with bleeding within the brain and head, damage the ability to absorb fluid and the high pressure causes further damage. The shunt keeps the pressure within reasonable limits.

The shunt is made of silicone and stainless steel or related materials and opens when the present pressure is reached. It can fail, become plugged up or infected and have to be replaced. They last for an indeterminate length of time. During long periods of time, the shunt may become slowly plugged but the ability to absorb spinal fluid may improve so it is possible that a shunt may fail but produce no symptoms. It is relatively uncommon for this to occur perfectly but can occur with minimal symptoms until something else de-compensates the system- then the shunt may have to be replaced.

The fluid is drained into the peritoneal cavity where it is absorbed. This is the space, which surrounds the stomach and most of the other abdominal organs. In the past, shunts were occasionally placed into the organ itself but didn't work well. Sometimes they're placed into a vein.

They are a fairly common microsurgical procedure and the valves and materials have improved substantially over the years.

Hope this gets your questions answered.

Michael J. Rosner, M.D.

Chapter 18

HOW WILL WE LIVE?

Joe Lupini had contacted an old friend and Property Manager, Abe Pheffer of Gummernick Properties and arranged an apartment for Bonnie and myself. I used to refer to that property as little Saigon because Vietnamese mainly occupied the complex. At any rate, it was definitely a depressed area but we had no choice but to call it home.

The first night there for Bonnie was horrific to say the least! The apartment was over run with cockroaches and camel crickets and by the next morning she wanted to abandon ship and frankly, I did not blame her.

Again, it was Joe Lupini to the rescue. He arranged to have my friends, David Anderson, Tim Howell and Lemuel Kidd, from Parliament Termite and Pest Control, to visit and treat for the insects. What a nightmare!

There was one final problem with no answer in site. How was I going to pay for the apartment not to mention pay the bills and buy groceries? My family had telephoned every charitable organization possible but to no avail. From Goodwill Industries to the United

Way there were no helping hands extended! Frankly, that explains my callous attitude today when approached for donations for such groups.

Although one church did donate thirty-five dollars it was hardly enough to meet our needs. We were down to water and grits when one afternoon came a knock at the back door. I found my way to the door only to find Joe Lupini, Lemuel Kidd, Tim Howell and David Anderson with twelve bags of groceries and even one bag full of popcorn. Needless to say, my eyes were full of tears and from that day forward, thanks to Joe, we were never in need for food or money!

When I had stepped down from regional manager to salesman along with that move came a drastic change in my pay scale. However, before the change could be started, I had the brain hemorrhage. The insurance company wanted to pay my disability claim but only on my new salary. This time it was Joe Galleger and Ray News at the corporate headquarters that went to bat for me and threatened to cancel all eighteen offices if they did not live up to my claim with my regional manager's salary. That percentage netted me a take home check of nine hundred forty nine and twenty-three cents each month.

I remember receiving my first check and the relief it brought! However, it also created problems in that it was the only money coming in and my life style prior to my illness was now catching up with me. My delinquent child support, failure to pay my taxes and bills, coupled with my medical bills, it was a wonder I was not in jail.

Bonnie finally got a job to help out. One day, after I had gotten my disability check, to celebrate our newfound wealth, we went to a Golden Skillet for lunch! Joe Lupini had taken me to his bank to cash my check and we were in hog heaven! However, by the time we got home I discovered my money was gone! It quickly dawned on me I had left my money envelope on the dinner table at the restaurant.

Frantically, we rushed back to the store knowing our monthly income was taken and we would even be deeper in an endless pit. However, upon our arrival, we learned an employee had found our money and turned it into the store manager who in turn had placed our money into his safe until the owner returned! Wow! Needless to say it restored my faith in humanity and made me realize how much I needed to change and return to clean living. I did not know it then but my trip back into the main stream of clean living had already begun.

As bad as it seemed, there were plenty more *Unforeseen Occurrences* to take place. Like the biblical story of Job, it finally would be even more unbelievable!

J. Lee Gilbert

Chapter 19

MY VISION RETURNS!

One morning around two o'clock, I was not sleeping when I began to see a light in my bedroom! To me, it was very bright, almost to the point of blinding. Since I was supposed to be blind, I thought I was dreaming! I yelled for help and Bonnie woke only to confirm I was awake and laying beside a window. Outside, the window there was a strong street light burning confirming we were witnessing a miracle! The light was actually hurting my eyes and we were jubilant!

That morning at exactly nine o'clock, we telephoned the Medical College of Virginia's Associated Physicians with the news! They did not believe it and ask to bring me in right away!

Upon my arrival, Dr. John Harbison examined me and in amazement he confirmed the slight return of my vision. Nothing was clear to me and even normal house lights were blinding but the fact remained my vision was returning! Needless to say, as the medical profession confirmed, it was truly a miracle!

Within six weeks, I was able to see twenty/ twenty straight ahead. There were several new problems now and how I was to overcome them was beyond my knowledge. Now I had no peripheral vision and although I could see, I was no longer able to read or write!

The doctors ran a variety of tests on my visual field and even had special glasses made for me. However, I learned by trial and error, just to turn my head and to remember I did not have any peripheral vision. It took a number of years to finally understand my visual limitations and how to compensate. Even today, twenty years later, I am still knocking things over and even an occasional fall. Maneuvering in large crowds proves to be a real challenge.

I have long since developed a technique to cope with my visual problem and in fact became so proficient with it I have the best driving record in the company in which I work today. My dear friend, Joe Lupini, owns that company.

Next was learning to read and write again. The stroke caused the loss of my left hand so I began to train my right hand how to print. At the same time, I began learning how to recognize words since my visual field was considerably reduced. I started a small notebook and as I built my reading vocabulary, I would add new words to my notebook.

During the day, when everyone had left the house, I would take a two to three mile walk to clear my head and strengthen my body. One afternoon a large blue van pulled along side of me to offer a ride and it was Hal Lowe, owner of Lowe Rid-O-Pest Company.

That day he offered me a job should I fully recover, to just pick up the phone and the job would be mine. The offer, later, would play a very important role in my life in the future.

The immediate concern was my home life and it was becoming more and more apparent it was the wrong life for me. Bonnie's son, Jim, had almost ruined my sports car and her daughter, Jan, kept the streets hot and was always on the phone when she was at the house. Then there was the constant yelling and arguing. The doctors had warned me to stay calm but that was impossible in this household.

It all came to a boil on a Saturday afternoon around five in the evening. Some tough looking biker came to the door looking for Jim to use his head for a mop and his butt for a broom! I assured him I wished Jim were here and our conversation resulted in a pretty good friendship.

Soon after that ordeal was through, another one erupted. This time I was trying to rest upstairs and the commotion began. I went downstairs to learn our phone bill had arrived with five hundred ninety four dollars worth of long distance calls on it! My stepdaughter, Jan, had been calling her boyfriend, Steve, who was in California! My disability check was only for nine hundred forty nine dollars and twenty-three cents each month and now most of that was gone and I exploded!

After I expressed my anger I stormed out of the house in a rage.

Behind me ran Jim and his friend, Brent, chasing me and promising to stomp me into the ground! At this point, I ran to escape harm since my health at the time would not allow for a fistfight. I ended up sleeping at the next-door neighbor's house until the next day when I returned to collect my things. I returned a few days later but determined to leave as soon as it was possible.

Leaving Bonnie would be the beginning of a very long up hill climb back to normalcy. Like the Biblical personage, Job, I had bottomed out and now the long journey to the top was about to begin and along the way would be many *Unforeseen Occurrences*.

Chapter 20

FREE AT LAST

I remember the morning that I ask Dr. John Harbison for permission to drive again. He looked as if he had seen a ghost and then started laughing. He explained I was lucky to be alive and for me not to even mention ever driving because it was never going to happen! I explained my livelihood depended on my driving which brought up my next request to return to work. "My God you are insane man!" was his reply.

After several more visits and examinations, reluctantly, Dr. Harbison gave permission to obtain a diver's license and permission to return to work. Of course, I was very apprehensive even though I was only allowed to return part time so I could be tested. Now, twenty-one months later, I was returning to the secular world and not aware of how much it had changed.

At this point, one more major change needed to be made. I searched through the newspaper and finally found a suitable room to rent from a nice old lady named Virginia McClure. Virginia had a poodle named Jock that later inspired one of my poems in my third book called *Reflections In Poetry*. The poem's title is *Otis*.

Virginia proved to be a major influence in my life.

Now I needed to wait for an appropriate time to move and begin a new life free from Bonnie and all that went with her. That time came soon enough when Bonnie and her sisters planned a trip to South Hill, Virginia. From the moment they left, I started packing up and moving out. By three p.m. I was long gone and left neither note nor hint where I might have gone. Like Martin Luther King once said: "free at last, thank God all mighty, free at last!"

After settling in at Virginia's, I went out for my groceries which was pathetic, to say the least but I had no choice. My food consumption mainly consisted of potted meat; vienna sausage; peanut butter; jam and various Campbell's soups. I had very little money due to my medical bills and child support and my return to work meant starting at the bottom. Nonetheless, I was very happy because I knew there was only one direction I could go and that was up!

For weeks I just stayed in my room and practiced reading. I chose to learn to read again on the Bible. From front to back several times and as I read I developed a notebook of new words. Next to each word I wrote how to pronounce them and their meaning. Within a few months I learned to recognize enough words to cover for my inability to read.

Even today, twenty years later, I have extreme difficulty recognizing words in print. Even more amazing, to me is, often I can hand write a poem and then am unable to read what I've written.

In fact, I enrolled into a night school for the purpose of learning how to recognize the written word. One night I had a speaking engagement at the school. The instructor approached me to inquire of my preparation, when I informed him I was ready. I also told him I could not read and he looked like he was going to have a heart attack. I explained not to worry because I had memorized my speech word for word just in case I developed a problem in my reading. Later that night, he was absolutely amazed because I accomplished my speech without a hitch!

Before long Virginia and I developed a strong bond. She used to tell her family and friends I was the neatest man she had ever met in her seventy-six years. However, when she discovered, what my diet consisted of she had a fit and brought that to an end immediately. From that moment on she would cook the best meals and it began to show on my waistline. In fact, my weight increased to two hundred thirty eight pounds.

There was one final hurdle and that was my job. By the time I was ready to return to work nothing remained the same. The greatest changes were the people. In my opinion the world had gone straight to hell! It was a dog eat dog world and it was very evident at Parliament. Before long I regretted returning to work. I had been assigned the most depressed area in our territory where the economy was so poor no one was buying anything. I felt I was given this assignment just to get me out of the way.

There were sales employees now that knew very little about the business. In fact, there was a salesman named Chuck Pearl that had no clue of how to tell the truth.

We had a training program set up in Petersburg, Virginia for The Great Atlantic Agency and at the meeting Chuck explained the biology of a German cockroach in which he stated a roach could live four years on a gram from a cracker. I almost had a heart attack! Actually, the German roach life expectancy is about eleven months.

At the office I went straight to Joe, my boss, to let him know about the lies being told in order to sell accounts. I was received well but later I learned it was only to patronize me. Things had really changed and I did not want any part of it. Secretly, I planned to leave the company after my discovery.

During my time at Parliament, I was able to secure some major accounts in the depressed territory of Petersburg that had been assigned to me. My first major break came when I was able to sell the John Randolph Hospital in Hopewell! I had worked on the account for a number of months and the sale meant I still had the ability to land the big account!

I remember the excitement and my drive back to the Richmond office. I could not wait to put the contract on Joe's desk as if to say "and you thought I was washed up!" But not so fast! I had already forgotten that my real boss did not work like that! In my heart, I was working for my Creator.

Ironically, just as I was approaching The Medical College of Virginia, just to my left off interstate 95, I began to feel very strange. Almost as if I were going to have another brain hemorrhage, I felt flushed and weak and as if I were about to pass out. I pulled over in an effort to regain my composure and as if the events were being controlled by a higher power a state police officer pulled up just in time! He approached my vehicle with caution until he heard my plea for assistance. Briefly, I explained my medical history and current feelings. The officer personally assisted me into his car and in a flash we were at the Medical College of Virginia in the emergency room.

Soon, I was wired up, so to speak and rushed to a room for what proved to be a fourteen day visit at which time the medical professionals finally explained what I was to expect as an aftermath of my brain hemorrhage and my shunt implant. The shunt basically relieves the pressure in my brain and acted as a value or by pass and released in my stomach. That process, that I had just experienced, happened often and left me feeling washed out.

Finally, because of the implant, I experienced seizures and although I am no medical expert, trust me; my explanation of the ordeal is simplistic to say the least.

After my much-needed medical orientation, I was released with a better understanding of what I could expect and subsequently, I was able to deal successfully with my future medical needs.

As proof that my luck was changing and my debt had been paid in full, to God, that is, out of the blue I received a call from Les Smith, the Manager at Lowe-Rid-O-Pest. Les would have a profound effect on my life in a good way for which even today I feel indebted. Les offered and I accepted a job that I have held for twenty years and helped me get back to and beyond my original place in life. Now the unexpected and *Unforeseen Occurrences* were becoming positives.

It is my conclusion, based on experience, if you practice good, good will return to you two fold!

Chapter 21

MY PRISON SENTENCE BEGINS

I started my new job at Lowe-Rid-O-Pest making less than I started making in nineteen sixty-seven. Les assured me and I knew it was true, give myself two years and I would return to and exceed the level I had reached at the time of my illness. It was almost two years to the day his statement proved true!

Although I had gainful employment, my job required regular use of a vehicle, which meant constant pressure on me due to my lack of peripheral vision. In a sense, it was a blessing in disguise because it gave me opportunity to practice and perfect my newly acquired disability.

At the end of those two years, Les announced his departure from the company. I was devastated because my role model was leaving just when I was riding high again. It proved to be another blessing in disguise and years later I became convinced someone else had been in control of my future. Again I had forgotten an old friend that I had worked for full time for a number of years and apparently he was still in control of my life but in a new way.

At Les' departure, another door opened for me. Hal Lowe, owner of Lowe Rid-O-Pest, offered me Les' job, which meant a large raise and more privileges. I accepted the position and it appeared there was a light at the end of the tunnel. But not so fast! Apparently, there were more dues to be paid and The Big Guy planned on collecting!

One day during one of my training programs, my secretary interrupted me. When I reached the front office, there were two state police officers baring bad news! Seems my ex-wife had collected A.D.C. (aid to dependant children) during my twenty-one month illness and now it was time to start paying it back. I was devastated! The total amount due by this point was sixty four thousand dollars; not counting the current charges that added four hundred dollars each month. It was time to start paying for all my neglect toward my children and my responsibility to the Creator.

By now I had cleaned up my mind and had developed a clean conscience using the Bible as my guide. Obviously, it was not complete and The Big Guy was putting me to the test. Years later, I wrote a poem called *The Big Guy* that appeared in my third book. It was a term I found myself using often during my trip back to a normal life. Even today in my *Writer's Work Shops,* I use the term frequently.

For several days I slept restlessly, very worried over how was I to survive on one hundred and sixty seven dollars a week. One day, I was leaving the house when I had a brainstorm! I pulled over my truck and with my whole heart and soul I prayed for help. I literally begged for guidance to direct me so I might over come this mountainous obstacle. After my prayer, I decided to stop at the first business I came to and apply for a second job.

That business happened to be a Crown gas station, which would be perfect. I turned in and talked with the manager, Sarah Sikes but they had no openings. I was not discouraged and filled out an application. That was on a Wednesday. When Friday rolled around something amazing occurred! Again I stopped to ask about the job only to learn one of her employees had to leave unexpectedly and there was an immediate need for a new employee. She asked me to start the next day on Saturday and I was astonished!

All of a sudden my prayer was answered and it appeared my problem was solved. However, my test was just beginning and it was to last nine and a half years. Just long enough to test, toughen and develop a cold and callus heart and attitude. Although along the way I would meet my dream come true that *Unforeseen Occurrence* that serves as my backbone today.

To this day, I often wonder about God and how it seems just when all is lost, a light will shine and directs you in the right direction. Be mindful though, it does not work for the callus heart!

J. Lee Gilbert

Chapter 22

VENGENCE IS MINE

Shortly after my new life of two full time jobs began, I sat down and figured out how old I would be at the end of my prison sentence, as I often referred to my two job commitment to pay back to the state; $64,000.00, not to mention the hospital bills. It would last nine and a half years, bringing it to an end in September 1995. I would only be forty-six years old and would have plenty of time left for a full life.

During this time of soul searching, it dawned on me I was a physical wreck. If I was to be successful in my endeavor the time was now that I should get in shape!

So, I started to exercise and run. It was really pathetic and at times even funny. I could hardly do ten push-ups or even run three hundred yards. After all, by this time I weighed two hundred thirty eight pounds and was absolutely over weight and out of shape.

I had moved from Virginia's, into an efficiency. In fact, Bonnie and I had tried to live together one more time but to no avail. Because of her, I had committed to a townhouse apartment but she only stayed three days leaving me with an empty apartment and another large responsibility.

The rent was twice that of the efficiency and it made things even more difficult. For almost a year, I lived in a very large empty apartment but with all of that I was very happy. Somehow, I knew there was light at the end of the tunnel for me. If only I could keep my eyes on the prize!

It became a matter of being busy and in doing so, I threw myself into fitness. My goals were to lose weight and to muscle up! By keeping my mind and body busy, there was no room for discouragement.

At the end of my lease period I secured a more affordable apartment and now was set to fulfill my prison sentence. Finally too, I was prepared for pay back which led to more *Unforeseen Occurrences* that taught me a valuable lesson that I will carry for the rest of my life.

What about the pay back? In a warped manner of thinking, I blamed women for my fate. In reality, I was simply reaping what I had sown. At any rate, I was determined to do to women what they had done to me. Truth is, I wanted to find that proverbial needle in a haystack, and a girl I could trust that would be my best friend, pal and confidante.

For years both men and women have been led to believe the best place to meet Mr. Right is in the bars, which is what I believed. In reality, the best place is at a grocery store! However, it did not take long to discover meeting girls at a gas station was like dipping your hands into a gold mine! Needless to say, I took full advantage!

My first year at Crown, I dated eighty-seven girls! I was a fully prepared cowboy with a stud service frame of mind. My best friend at the time, Tommy Goode, constantly warned me saying, "Keep your hands over your pockets" but I paid no attention. It did not take long to learn and I soon developed a policy: women are only interested in two things, themselves and what I could do for them!

Tommy was a story all by himself. Actually, he was a loner with no friends and really didn't want any. He had worked part time at Crown for many years and truly felt like friends will use, abuse and accuse you too. However, for reasons unknown to me, Tommy seemed to attach himself to my ways and me. That was perfect for me until out of the blue he was arrested for credit card fraud.

I had been aware of his thievery and for several years tried to mend his ways but to no avail. Of course, "whatever a man is sowing is also what he shall reap" and Tommy finally reaped his reward. From the night of his arrest to my last day at Crown, Tommy remains to be a major influence throughout my *Unforeseen Occurrence!*

At this point please note, because there were so many females, I elected to only share a few of the stories. My hope is that readers will reap rewards from my story and not travel down the same path I chose. My story ends in heavenly bliss but for most it is disastrous.

Chapter 23

LOVE THEM AND LEAVE THEM!

For the first time in my life, I was forced to work two jobs, one of which was below my dignity! It was time to learn how the rest of the world lived and eventually add to my bank of life's experiences.

On my first day I showed up at Crown looking and acting like a banker, which would not last long. It was fast pace and required some real holding power. Actually, it was good because I was forced into humility, another quality I desperately needed.

My first night alone at the gas station was truly a memorable one! It was bitterly cold and I almost froze! I worked in a small island house with two doors that open out on both sides. When the customer finished pumping their gas, they came to the island house to pay and usually two at a time and each held the door open until they paid leaving me with a large draft and constantly cold. By the time I arrived home I felt like a block of ice!

The next day when I returned to Crown I informed Tommy of my experience. At that time he began to educate me on the value of insolated clothing. Of course, I had to endure one more night of severe cold but the next day I was at the local A & N store to purchase the things Tommy informed me of including insolated boots. Needless to say, I did not have another frozen night as my growing and learning continued to mount I fed my mind on the principles of positive thinking. I concentrated on the works of Zig Ziglar and Norman Vincent Peale to keep me focused.

The winter nights at crown were very cold and lonely. It provided a perfect back ground for me to write and write is what I did. With each experience came one more inspiration after another.

I will begin with Shannette, a beauty queen from Roanoke with a lot of secrets, of course, unknown to me. She was an important person with a very good company, Richmond Cold Storage, which is where we met. Before long we became very close and she moved into my apartment lock, stock and barrel, so to speak.

When I was at work for Crown, she too was there and had learned my job so well she filled in for me when I had errands to run. However, my life was an open book and I had learned through experience, it was the best way to be. I had no secrets and no need for cover up. Subsequently, I did not need to try constantly to remember each cover up story. As a result, I would *Sleep With A Clean Conscience,* the title of a poem I wrote that appeared in my first book. Often times Shannette had the run of my apartment and soon I would learn that was a big mistake because curiosity got the best of her.

Gradually, I noted a mood change in Shannette and one evening

I ask what was the problem. Although it took awhile to get her to spill the beans, the truth was very hard to bear. It seems while I was at work she had been reading my diaries. I have been keeping a diary since nineteen seventy and kept a record of everything in my life and I mean everything!

Needless to say, we had a real knock down drag out argument. I explained my life had been an open book to her but her life was all kept in a closet. I had never intended for her or anyone else to rummage through my dairies. I had trusted her and now I learn she had breached that trust. My final point to her, I knew nothing about her, for the most part.

Frankly, what a person did before I met them, to me, was just water under the bridge. It is more important what the person is right now.

I started my diaries as a form of release and a record for reflections when I got older. By that time, I could review them and remember my youth the good and bad times of my life. My third book in fact was called *Reflections In Poetry* and was based on many of the details found in my diaries.

After a few days of sulking she sat me down and spilled the beans so to speak. Number one, she had been married for two years to a black man! Although now divorced, she had an even greater revelation!

Just before our relationship, she had a friend that too was

married to a black man. He had a fantasy, to be intimate with another white woman while his wife watched! What a sick mind. Of course, Shannette agreed and was victimized more than once. She explained in detail how they got her stinking drunk and then had a good time with her body. She explained it was the only way she could perform their request but it did not matter to me. In my opinion, if she had no more respect for herself than that how could I believe she had learned her lesson and would not return to that life again? Needless to say, it was all over between us and I was slowly becoming cold and callus!

The stories are endless and this book could be equal in size to an encyclopedia, if I were to reveal all the bad relationships that I had been involved in after my illness. However, for the sake of proof, I will continue with a few more not to brag but to prove how foolish such a life is and how it can only lead to pain, sorrow and frustration.

During my first year of two full time jobs, I was able to date eighty-seven girls! The first ten or eleven were married and I did not know it but discovered each by mistake, sad but true.

In nineteen eighty-seven, at Lowe Rid-O-Pest, we hired a young lady and former police office named Lisa. Of course, it was my job to train her and during the course of our ride together, she discovered my plight and decided to find Miss Right for me! Yea, right!

One day while working a job, J. W. Ferguson Company, Lisa came running to me claiming to have found the right woman for me. She introduced me to Susan Powers and the roller coaster ride was about to begin.

We dated four or five months primarily on weekends. However, I began to notice Susan would just disappear for three or four days at a time only to re-emerge as though she had been around all along.

For the most part, when we were together we sat around her apartment smoking and joking, drinking and stinking as my friend, David Anderson, used to say. She also loved to bowl so whenever she was in town on the weekends we would bowl ourselves crazy.

This went on for a while until I confronted her about her disappearing act only to learn she was burning a candle from both ends. She was also dating some one that lived in Northern Virginia and so once again I got the shaft and became even more callus because I did not want to share my relationship with anyone else. Again, I brought the relationship to an abrupt end.

Then one day while responding to an emergency call for Lowe Rid-O-Pest, I met a beautiful girl named Silvia Wilks. She managed an ambulance service and was single. We seemed to have a lot in common and whatever time was available to me I spent with Silvia.

One Saturday afternoon, we had a cook out and I ended up

spending the night. Late in the evening she asked me to marry her over and over again. Finally, in the heat of the moment, I said yes and was in heaven again or so I thought!

I left early the next day because I had to go to work at Crown by six a.m. in the morning. In the excitement, I told Tommy, my best friend at the time, all about Silvia and he thought I was crazy and wasting my life and emotions. I was soon to learn what Tommy thought would soon come true. He would say: "Women are only interested in two things; themselves and what you can do for themselves"! Soon I adopted that philosophy for myself.

At any rate, Silvia showed up at eleven a.m., with some devastating news! That morning she had gotten a phone call from her former fiancé and he had a change of heart and wanted to marry her and she accepted! Unbelievable and I was crushed! How could she ask me to marry her the night before and then accept a plea from her former fiancé to marry him?

Needless to say, Tommy rubbed it in and went on and on saying, "I told you so" for weeks. I was turning into a cold and callus male. From that point on, I aimed to love them and leave them and no desire for a commitment. From nineteen eighty seven to nineteen ninety-five it had become my lot in life but there was light at the end of the tunnel but I would not see it until the end of nineteen ninety-eight. This time an *Unforeseen Occurrence* that would change my life for the good forever!

Chapter 24

ONE MORE TRY

I needed to clear my brain of negative thoughts and it was time for some soul searching. I telephoned the kids and planned a visit and to stay a few days hoping I would return with a new mood and a new attitude.

My son played in a successful band called *Red Totem Idol* and it happened that they were playing at a popular nightclub that weekend. Earlier I had been playing guitar with Kevin when he ask me if I would join them on stage Saturday night to play *Lonely Man*, a song he had written and we used to play together. Reluctantly, I agreed and it proved to be one of those *Unforeseen Occurrences* that I will never forget.

The club was packed and I was the only cowboy there. Kevin introduced me as his hero and mentor and I felt like a billion dollars! When I went on stage around eleven o'clock that evening, it was I that started the song and it was only Kevin and I playing the first verse. The rest of the band joined us for the remainder of the song.

When I left the stage, we got a standing ovation and I was high as a kite and ready to take on the world! At that point, if I had died, I would have died the happiest and proudest father in the universe. I returned home with a clear mind and renewed spirit.

That next Thursday evening around 10 p.m., a lady friend stopped for gas and to say hello. Months earlier, she had tried to start a relationship with me but I informed her if she lost about a hundred pounds she might have a chance. She had even sent anonymous roses to the station for which most of the guys made fun of me. Later I wrote a poem called Secret Flowers which appeared in my third book called; *Reflections In Poetry* and was inspired by that event.

At any rate, there were two other girls in the car that caught my attention, one of which had a "male bashing attitude" named Teri Bland and the other a beautiful redhead! Of course, I got the phone number of Ms. Attitude, which led me to some good times and some very bad times.

The very next night, I called Ms. Attitude, only to have a black man to answer and needless to say I decided not to call again. However, that was not to be the end of the matter.

About a month later, on a Wednesday night, Teri showed up again looking very tired and with a cigarette in her mouth. She explained she ran a day care and the black man that answered her phone was there to pick up his child. That made sense to me and I promised to call at her request.

That call came on Sunday evening and it lasted two hours, as was each call every night afterward. It looked like my dream come true was about to come but only time would tell.

I learned Teri's experience with men had been the same as mine with women. In fact, her ex-husband had left her for another man only after she found pictures and videos of him with other men. Repulsive, to say the least, so with both back grounds being similar, it seemed reasonable we were bound to work. After all, both of us had traveled the same path.

Teri had two boys named James and Dan and from the start we hit it off! The boys were a real pleasure and I made it my goal to teach them all I could, even offering and giving pest control classes for their schools on several occasions. My boss and good friend, Joe, was proud to have me speak at the schools in fact all over Virginia.

In time, I became active with the Konawa Youth Football League, where Teri was on the Board of Directors and ran the concession stand. We would arrive on game days at six in the morning and worked often until ten at night. After my first year the football league offered me a coach's job, which I accepted and I hit the ground running!

The boys began to copy me in everything. I was lifting weights so they had to have their own weights. I ran for my health and they would join me. I dressed western so they had to have cowboy hats and boots too. I rode a bike for health and they were right with me riding theirs too. Teri joined us and it seemed perfect.

I began to teach the boys and show them little tricks that would help them through life such as personal hygiene to marshal arts. They became proficient with each skill I taught even mastering checkers. We were having a ball! Sad to say, while I was having a ball with someone else's children, my own kids went without.

On certain evenings, I worked at a Crown gas station. Teri and the boys would ride their bikes up to the station to visit. I even taught the boys how to run the register and the customers would play along. Everything seemed perfect.

As for Teri and me, we took a few vacation trips alone and I was sure she was finally the right one for me. The time came for me to pop the question and she accepted. After all, countless women had shafted me and her ex-husband left her for another man! You would think that scenario would produce a perfect marriage.

We took several trips together that provided time to get to know each other while her parents would watch the boys.

Our first trip was short but full of excitement and good memories. Hootie and the Blowfish were on top of the record charts so we had stopped for a copy of their latest release and cranked it up loud and had a ball all the way to a bed and breakfast lodge in the heart of the historic district of the Statler Brothers home town of Stanton, Virginia.

Since our relationship initially was full of such like ventures, my conversation with others, unfortunately, reflected it. Thank God that today I have become more discreet.

The wedding was quaint, short and simple! The Kanawha football league provided the honeymoon gaieties and we stayed at the Berkley Motel in downtown Richmond, Virginia and everything was perfect. Teri even surprised me with a Berkley Motel, first class robe for memories sake.

The room was the motel's bridal suite and it came fully equipped with wine, king size bed and a Jacuzzi! The first night was full of sexual encounters and heavenly bliss too numerous to detail and unfortunately it was long forgotten by nineteen ninety-eight!

After the honeymoon, it was down to family life. We had a big yard sale in Colonial Heights, where Teri's parents lived and where we were able to consolidate our belongings and create a single household. The yard sale was a huge success and we were off to a great start.

Then came another millstone for me and it was big! For nine and a half years I had worked two full time jobs and now comes a letter from the state of Virginia announcing my prison sentence was finally over and I was free at last! It proved to be perfect timing for I had no idea when the sentence would be over!

Needless to say, Teri and I partied hardy all that weekend!

However, I had grown so accustom to working two full time jobs for a brief time I was actually afraid to give up my part time job. Finally I did and it took literally months to adjust.

Part of that adjustment would include a real vacation, my first since the late seventies and Teri's absolute first. We planned to visit the Dutch Country, Hershey and Mr. Roger's Neighborhood in Pennsylvania.

We started our trip with a stop in Washington D.C. and took a tour of the Capital to visit the historical sites. Due to our late departure from Washington we decided to sleep over in Philadelphia. The next morning we left early but the motel had trouble with my debit card. After trying my card four times the fifth seemed successful and we were on our way.

Upon our arrival in Hershey we discovered we only had twenty-seven dollars left in our account. We were devastated and spent our last dollars trying to find out what happened to our savings. Seems every time the clerk in Philadelphia tried our card automatically the money was deducted and yet the clerk did not know and so he would repeat the process until my account had been erased. It took all day and part of the next to straighten out the mess. Obviously, the trip was almost perfect and everyone thought we were the perfect couple. You never saw one without the other and for all intents and purposes it was true.

In early nineteen ninety-eight came one final honor! I had been nominated for Father of the Year by the State of Virginia! After all, as a stepfather, I taught kids classes on insects; a football coach; soccer and baseball dad and full time parent. I felt like a million dollars the day I got the award and thought I was on top of the world.

Name a mother that would not have been proud of their husband that had successfully adopted their true father's role and had managed to do so smoothly and successfully? You would think a lady would be happy and proud to have married a man with such qualities!

But not so fast! Remember, whatever a man is sowing this he shall also reap and although I was cleaning up, there was still some dirty laundry I had to take care of therefore some more *Unforeseen Occurrences* left to go.

J. Lee Gilbert

Chapter 25

MONKEY WRENCH

Just when life seemed perfect then came a monkey wrench! Teri began talking about my duel personalities and my "Jeckel and Hyde" ways. Neither the boys nor I had a clue what she was talking about. However, in a letter she wrote to me, and in response to a note to her, she confessed the reverse was true. In her letter, dated, August twenty seventh, nineteen ninety-five she confessed: "Yesterday I felt like everyone was ganging up on me and so I gave into frustration, depression and anger instead of fighting the feelings, I fought the boys and myself and you. That was wrong. I am going to try very hard to practice these things. Not to let the negative activities that might be going on around me affect my happiness. I have never in my life been so happy and it's because of you. We have so much to look forward to and to be thankful for and I love you". Her words proved to be empty.

At the same time she was in a feud with her sister, Maude, and I encouraged her to formulate a dialogue with her. Maude and her husband were very well off and I could tell there was a degree of jealously between Teri and Maude. Some years earlier Maude and

Teri had a serious disagreement over some race tickets. They had an argument that lead to closing the door on communication. After months of conversation about the subject, Teri finally wrote Maude and to her surprise, Maude telephoned and they were off and running. You would think that was perfect but it really was the beginning of the end for us.

Soon Teri approached me about opening her own checking account separate from my money. It became apparent to me something was up but she was not talking. The closeness we once enjoyed was not there and the sad part was I had no clue why.

At work and elsewhere, I did not let it be known because whether on the football field or out socially, everyone thought we were the perfect couple! We were the perfect example of that old expression, the calm before the storm and when the storm hit everyone, including me, were caught off guard. No one expected it and it hit like a ton of bricks!

We were planning a trip to go see Teri's sister, Maude, in South Carolina. Then one evening just before the trip, Teri broke the news to me! She would be making the trip alone. I was shocked and explained her old car could not make the trip. Undaunted, she prepared to depart showing no emotion at all. I did not know it at the time but she had rented a car and made the trip on our mortgage payment! What a fool I proved to be.

The morning arrived for her departure; Teri and the boys were gone as if it were just another day, leaving another fool behind that refused to read the handwriting on the wall.

For whatever reason, generally speaking, people in love are unable to see the writing on the wall. Not once but many times before I had been down this street but still I was unable to face reality. It is a denial factor clouded by emotions. Only time and experience can mold a person into making the right decision and even then the lesson is ignored.

Another *Unforeseen Occurrence* was about to take place. Although devastating, at the time, it ended up being a real blessing in disguise. During the next few days, I did some real hurting and soul searching and unknowingly preparing for the devastating news.

Teri and the boys arrived late Sunday night with no time for conversation. However, the following day all hell broke loose! Teri asks me to move out because we needed some time apart. Neither the boys nor I understood but there was no changing her mind. Somehow, I knew before the words came out of her mouth.

Ashamed of the fact, I kept the events happening at home to myself and began to hypocritically act as though I had the best family arrangement a man could possibly have although I was like the proverbial "white washed grave," "outwardly it is beautiful but inside full of dead men's bones"!

I went to an old friend, Bruce Harding, manager of the Willis

Companies and ask for an apartment and swearing him to silence. Teri had ask me not to move far away because she hoped we could reunite and like a fool I said fine.

The day came for me to move and Teri did everything possible to assist. At the time I thought she was being very fair and I thought she did want to save our marriage. In fact, after my move was complete, she allowed the boys to spend a few nights with me.

What a fool! Every morning I would prepare for work and before going, I would stop at Teri's to wake her. After all, I had a key but that did not last long. Although my fight against being a deadbeat dad was over and won, I had many opportunities to galvanize my relationship with my children but I elected to continue chasing an elusive dream called women! Even in a no win situation, I continued to waste my time even though I knew the Creator kept score.

One Saturday another soccer game was scheduled and naturally, I planned to go with Teri and the boys only to learn I was supposed to meet them there instead. Upon my arrival, I discovered Teri, Dan, her former husband, and his parents were already there cozy as bugs in a rug. I was treated as though I had a communicable disease and needless to say for me it was the proverbial "straw that broke the camel's back"!

When I arrived at home, I immediately telephoned Teri and left a message that basically said she could kiss where the sun don't shine! The story was about to get very interesting as I was nearing the end of my downward spiral!

I learned later that Teri had recorded my message because I had cursed and that was not my forte'. It was just one more lesson I learned on my way back to the good life. Years ago my first sermon was entitled: *Use Your Tongue For Good* and now I felt like the Creator was teaching me that valuable lesson all over again. From the child support issue through my prison sentence every lesson proved to be a reminder of what the Creator had taught me years earlier on which I had turned my back. Pay back is hell!

J. Lee Gilbert

Chapter 26

LIVING A LIE

I spent the next few months living a lie leading people to believe my life was just perfect. On the weekends I spent my life at yard sales, flea markets and estate sales trying to rebuild my life and set up house keeping again. For the sake of the boys, I let Teri keep the best part of what we had developed.

In time, I noticed my Santa Claus suit was missing and realized I had left it in Teri's Mom's garage. Then I was really caught off guard when I discovered one of my diaries was missing too. I have been keeping a diary for years in fact since nineteen seventy-seven and each year it took two books to complete. I discovered the first half of nineteen ninety-eight was missing.

Since Teri had become so cold and callus, I was very concerned that either item would be returned. I telephoned to arrange a pick up of those items and left a message but never heard back until about three weeks later. What a turn of events that was to follow!

One Saturday while I was out washing my vehicles, Teri, the boys and her parents drove up. Teri got out with my Santa suit and a zip lock baggie in her hands. She was very cold and stern and gave them to me while at the same time threatening to call the police if I did anything to bother her! She also stated she had already notified the police about a potential problem with me. Can you imagine my reaction? It was one of complete dismay! I remained silent during the entire encounter.

At the same time, her mother got in my face also and in the worst possible tone and manner, pointing her finger at me and asked why I called her daughter a bitch? In view of what was happening there was no need for an answer because Teri was demonstrating before my very eyes the title I had given her. Not allowing a response from me, Teri told her mother to stop wasting her breath and without a word from me got into her rental car and drove off.

I did not know it then but by not replying to her threats, I created a great legal defense for me later. I did not see nor talk with Teri again until after the divorce.

You really never know someone until these circumstances. Then their true colors become apparent. Here are some cases in point.

One afternoon I got a call from Hecht's department store. I was so proud to have an account with this major chain of department stores. However, a very nice lady asks why all of a sudden I had stopped paying my bill. Hecht's is the only credit card of mine that Teri asked to keep and promised to pay faithfully. What a fool I was to believe her! She had not made one payment and to me it was a deliberate attempt to ruin my good credit standing. I made arrangements to bring it up to date and called Teri to ask for my credit card back. She never did make a payment and explained she had cut up the card and had made arrangements to pay twenty-five dollars a month, which was well below the minimum payment required. I paid the account off but Hecht's refused to continue my credit. Fortunately, when it came time to purchase my current house, my attorney and mortgage company were able to clear up Teri's attempts to ruin my credit.

Then there was a matter of insurance. The boys' father had insurance on them and I cancelled Teri's coverage after calling and leaving several messages to that effect. I was not about to continue payments for her coverage and informed her of my steps to remove her name from the insurance plan. However, during the entire legal process she continued to take the boys to various doctors and using my insurance card in an effort to postpone the payments on those bills. Finally, at a great expense to me, my attorney sent a letter of intent to prosecute to Teri's attorney in order to get her to stop the insurance fraud.

The divorce proved to be a real nightmare and the things I would learn along the way however, only served to strengthen me for a brighter future. Teri would continue to cause me a lot of grief for many months even after the divorce was final. However, the

Unforeseen Occurrence about to occur made it all worth the trip!

In September nineteen ninety six, a real strange turn of events occurred. For nine years I had worked at Parliament Pest Control and Joe Lupini was my boss. When I left, I went to work at Lowe Rid-O-Pest, which was owned by a mutual friend and I soon learned was a tyrant, Hal Lowe.

When, out of the blue, Mr. Lowe decided to sell the company because he and his ex-wife were at each other's throat over ownership and profits distribution, none other than my old friend, Joe Lupini, stepped up to the plate to buy it. To me, it was like throwing brother rabbit into the brier patch! For years I had struggled to keep my head above water and now my hard up hill climb was about to become smooth sailing.

A case in point was my pay scale. For years I served Mr. Lowe and only brought home one hundred sixty seven dollars a week because the rest of my earnings was confiscated by the State. After nine and a half years of slavery for pennies, the financial burden to the State had ended. Hal Lowe was very happy not because the weight had been lifted off me but because I got an automatic raise that did not cost him a red cent! That having been said, you can easily understand when I say that whenever you ran into Hal Lowe the first words out of his mouth were "what's your problem?" There was never a positive thought from that man!

Joe Lupini, on the other hand, was exactly the opposite. He had worked with me for years and knew I believed in letting your yes mean yes and your no, no! (Matthew 5: 37) So, right out of the starting block, Joe erased all the mundane and repetitious reporting Mr. Lowe had me doing and replaced it with positive production and a pay scale commensurate to the responsibility.

In fact, when Joe discovered the meager amount of my income, he had it adjusted accordingly. Finally, I began to feel that a higher force was in control of my life again. I offer only the following as evidence or proof. The *Unforeseen Occurrence* that made the whole trip worthwhile.

J. Lee Gilbert

Chapter 27

MY SAVING ANGEL

Upon purchase of the company, the first thing Joe did was change the name of the Company to Loyal Termite and Pest Control. During the course of the next few months, a phone call came in regarding one of our technicians named Chris Witt. Joe Lupini, his daughter, Kim and the sales representative, Gena, took the call and the customer was very upset and wanted to cancel our service.

In response to the call, the technician was taken off the job and it was a good practice to send the service supervisor to smooth over the damage and try to save the customer. Frankly, the technician and I had been at odds for many months but his bad service proved to be a beginning of my trip back to and beyond the best days of my life.

I arrived on a Tuesday morning at Chester Lake Apartments only to meet the most beautiful woman I had ever laid my eyes on! However, due to the events surrounding she and our technician, she was less than friendly. In fact, it took months to break the ice with her but what a wise investment of my time.

I returned to my office lit up like a Christmas tree! Of course, I shared my excitement with my best company friend Faye Taylor and from the start she encouraged me to ask Jennifer for a date. Each week that I went to service Chester Lake, Faye would ask "did you ask her?" and I would say, " no, I did not have the nerve". Of course, she would encourage me and I would continue to chicken out!

I should explain that Faye Taylor was the Company bookkeeper and often I would joke about chasing her around the block if our ages were more compatible. She and I shared the same office and along with it we shared a lot of secrets and other confidential matters. She was almost like an older sister to me.

Faye and I had become so close one day out of the blue, Hal Lowe came in and removed my office door and until this day the door has not been returned. In doing so, he had hoped to put an end to our confidential talk! Unknown to all, Faye was able to help me with my pay back.

At the same time, my son, Kevin, as mentioned in chapter twenty-four, was starting to make it big in music. He had a band called Red Totem Idol and they had released their second album and he had sent a copy to me via special delivery. Needless to say, I was very proud of my son's accomplishment and wanted everyone to know of his success, including Jennifer.

That next morning I went to Chester Lake with a smile on my

face that extended from ear to ear and proud of Kevin's album. Along with the album came newspaper and magazine releases too. This was just what I needed to break the ice with Jennifer! Kevin did not know it but it was because of him I was able to start a dialogue with her.

When I entered her office she could tell right away something was up and she ask what I was so excited about? I explained the whole story to her and we were off and running! I loaned her the album and she actually was smiling when I left. I went straight to a pay phone to call Faye and let her know the ice was broken and I was closer to asking Jennifer out than ever before!

The next week proved to be the beginning of the *Unforeseen Occurrence* that would change my life forever! Although for years my life had been like a roller coaster ride with a lot of serious downs, it was now turning into a ride through paradise. Today I truly believe in the Biblical promise: "Whatever a man is sowing this he will also reap" found at Galatians 6: 7,8.

For years I abandoned my responsibilities and for years I paid the price. Conversely, when I began to face my responsibilities, slowly they began to turn around and gradually it became almost impossible to have a bad day. A case in point was Jennifer.

That next Tuesday, Jennifer returned my album and I suggested we have lunch and maybe I could tell her some more about the band. If the truth were to be told, I was only using that as an excuse to be with her. She quickly accepted and a date was arranged. I could not wait to tell my friend Faye, so as soon as I left Jennifer's office, again I went straight to a phone to call her with the good news! "I never had any doubt", Faye said, in an encouraging tone. What a friend she proved to be.

However, when the date time arrived, again on Tuesday, her regular service day at the apartment complex, I was floored with a counter proposal! She did not have the time for lunch but ask if we could have dinner together and suggested Sunday evening at the Omni Motel Restaurant in downtown Richmond, VA. I thought I was going to have a heart attack from my excitement and could not contain myself until that evening. By this time my thoughts and feelings about Teri had turned cold and my new life was about to go into high gear!

Later that same day, Jennifer called and asked if she could come over on Wednesday night and of course I agreed. Over night my life began to change and it has been like paradise every since.

From the moment I left the ministry until this point, it had always been a struggle. Constant and gradual rise from the bottom only to be slammed with another *Unforeseen Occurrence* that would put me in the start over again mode!

If it were not women problems it was financial woes. Like the old song said: "gloom, despair and agony on me"! Imagine my relief and feelings of ecstasy when Jennifer stepped into the picture with her beautiful smile and supportive ways.

She arrived at my apartment at seven thirty five that evening and to quote my diary from nineteen ninety-eight: "had the most unbelievable night of my life"! She was so beautiful! Needless to say I was on cloud nine, whatever that means. We had shrimp cocktail and drank wine. We held hands and soon started kissing. Wow! It proved to be a night in my life I will never forget! When Jennifer left I could not contain myself because someone so beautiful chose to spend her time with me in such a romantic way. The remainder of that night I spent thinking about Jennifer and thinking how my life was turning around for the good.

The next day was Thanksgiving Day and I had a lot to be thankful for especially because of Jennifer. I did not know it then but the *Unforeseen Occurrence* that would change my life forever had taken place right before my eyes and I did not know it. From that day in November until now it has been one big party and in fact in my book called *Reflections In Poetry*, there is a poem called Life Of The Party Goes On, that pointed out that fact and was inspired by those events.

J. Lee Gilbert

Chapter 28

FINALLY ONE STEP AHEAD

In the spirit of good news and everything turning out perfect, from that night until now it continues to be like "life in a bed of roses"!

That weekend, Jennifer and I met at the Omni Motel Restaurant in the heart of Richmond, Virginia and it was like life in paradise! From the time I laid eyes on her that evening until she left my apartment at eight thirty that night it was pure heaven on earth. We were not at a loss for words all evening and in fact until this day that has been the case.

It was a classic date in that we were the only couple on the terrace sitting in dim lighting and the waiter was perfect and just attentive enough, not overly familiar.

Jennifer was dressed to kill; so to speak, in a dress secretly I wished I could see through. I learned later, she had left her home dressed to go skating and had stopped at a filling station to change only to repeat the process again before she returned home. At the time, I had no idea what she was going through just to spend time with me. If only I had known.

After our marriage, she told the whole story and I was so humbled and honored that she thought so much of me and would go through so much for me.

Her efforts to date me were full of such like experiences. For instance, one evening after leaving my apartment, she stopped at a Texaco gas station across the street for gas. She was running very late and in a hurry. She went to pay the attendant only to lock herself out of her car!

She ran back to my apartment for help crying and very upset, to say the least. It happened that I had a membership to AAA and telephoned for roadside service. I drove her back to her car and waited until she gained access and was off and running. Every time there was an event, I would fall deeper in love and closer to her.

Soon I learned the value of Jesus' words at Matthew 19: 5 when he stated: "that is why a man will leave his father and mother and cling to his wife and the two will become one flesh"! A thought I cherish because of Jennifer.

For the longest time, she seemed so sad and apprehensive about everything. As a result, it was a matter of calculating my steps so she would relax with me and emerge from her protective shell. Often I would give her a full body message and she was so tense it was like putting lotion on a two by four.

After several months of dating, Jennifer became very relaxed and always laughing and smiling. You would never see one without the other. In fact, at restaurants we would frequent the waitresses knew better than to seat us across from each other. Everyone considered us love bugs and I did not mind the reputation at all.

During those months, I told Jennifer about my ordeal with Teri and my nightmare during the brain hemorrhage and my need to work two full time jobs for nine and a half years and in turn, instead of causing her to run, it only served to strengthen her resolve to get closer to me. Because of the mess with Teri, she strongly urged me to employ an attorney and be prepared for a rough ride. Reluctantly, I ask Joe Lupini for the name of a good law firm and he suggested Leclair and Ryan. Eventually, Mike Tellus was assigned to my case and now I was sitting on go, so to speak, in case a legal war was to break out. Joe Lupini, my boss, even loaned me the money so I was poised for battle.

About two weeks to the day of that decision, I received a threatening letter from an attorney representing Teri and this time I was prepared at every turn. To this day, I still give full credit to Jennifer for forcing me to take the right steps and stop assuming everyone is good and will do the right thing. By phone, I left a voice mail with her attorney and even warned the lawyer to make sure she collected her fees in advance because Teri was not good at paying her bills. Also, I left my attorney's name and number and invited them to contact him. My attorney had warned me it would get nasty but I would not believe it. Finally, the evidence came that made me finally see these circumstances bring out the worst in people and Teri was no exception.

The joke was on Teri! She was shocked to learn I had already hired an attorney, which in turn let the air out of their sail, so to speak. There was no front they could attack that had not already been addressed. Their key issue was insurance, that I had already cancelled, but we made it clear I was not the sole provider for Teri's boys and in fact their own father was to bare that responsibility.

In the end, after a long fight and tremendous expense, we won the war. Sometimes, however, I wonder did I really win since the cost was so devastating. To this day I realize if I had not listened to Jennifer, the outcome would have been much different. Although that chapter of my life was through, that was not to be the end of the fight with Teri.

Please know circumstances are affected by a party's willingness to turn around and clean up his act. As for the individual who gives up or refuses to acknowledge error that person's fate will only worsen until complete failure.

To make a mistake or to choose to do wrong is one thing but to face up to a problem and plot a plan to correct it is quite another. To avoid your responsibility toward your children is not a position favored by the Creator of the universe. In fact, according to the

Bible at Luke 17: 2, "it would be like tying a millstone around your neck and being thrown into the sea". That is not a pleasant thought; therefore, to be a deadbeat dad only brings hardships unending!

At any rate, Jennifer and I were together every night and our love was growing stronger and stronger and I was finally realizing what I had worked for all my life and the "unforeseen occurrence that befall us all" had finally come around my way for the good.

December seventeenth, nineteen ninety-eight was different from most because it was the night I asked Jennifer to marry me. We had experienced one of the most intimate moments of my life and then I popped the question and her answer was as precious as they come: "all righty then"! I ask what kind of answer was that for the most important question a man could ask a woman? We laughed hardy and I then asked, what did I look like or sound like, some buckaroo from the sticks? After the laughter was over from that moment on until the day we married, I asked Jennifer to marry me everywhere we went! Every restaurant; shopping center; every special event; every show and at every shopping and historical landmark around the country I asked the question and got a resounding Yes! She asked why I kept asking a question she already said yes to and my response was she had no recourse when the day came but to say yes or I would sue her for breach of promise. Of course, I was joking.

During the next few months we started the process of planning a wedding event that would turn my life into paradise! I did not know it at the time but the *Unforeseen Occurrence* for my near future would change my way of living, my values and my life style for the better. Often I am reminded of Job in the Bible because his story soon became mine. The blessings were to be one hundred times that which I lost during my illness and subsequent nine and a half year struggle to normalcy.

Because of Jennifer, I believe there is no room for deadbeat dads! There is always a way to make up for the deficiency and to find happiness at the same time. It will not be perfect or easy but I believe where there is a will there is a way. My eventual marriage to Jennifer is proof.

Each of the planning stages involved more expenditure and by the time we were selecting a wedding gown I began to wonder where was the money coming from because I already knew my limits. However, I said nothing in fear of upsetting the apple cart.

Literally, we spent weeks just selecting a bridal gown. Jennifer tried on every dress at David's Bridal and frankly she looked like a model in all of them. At one point the manager ask and even suggested that she apply for a models job at her corporate head quarters. I was a typical male and was lapping it up like a kitten over a milk bowl.

In the end, Jennifer's gown cost right at one thousand dollars and secretly I was ready to have a cow! I had no clue how nor who was going to pay for all of this but I did know it was not going to be me!

The next concern was Jennifer's arrangements for a honeymoon. She started talking about a trip to Mexico and in an effort not to poor water on her sail I played along with the dream. Again though, privately, I thought where is all this money coming from because my bowl was empty. Then I wondered perhaps this woman was a little out of my league but kept the thoughts to myself in hopes she would run out of steam. A trip like the one she was planning would cost a fortune. It appeared to me again I would return to a two full time jobs life to pay for the wedding.

The straw that broke the camel's back came when she started talking about house hunting! To go house hunting was a joke to me. I had just cut off the ropes and broke the chains of two full time jobs and my nose was barely above the water. Besides that my apartment and subsequent divorce from Teri left me penniless. I finally sat her down and expressed my concerns and she finally spilled the beans and what a shock!

She had waited in an effort to make sure I was safe and not out to take advantage of her like most men, she explained. She wanted to be sure that I was legitimate and true to my word. According to her, most men are not truthful. I had news for her that females were just as bad! We laughed and agreed but I was still waiting for an explanation.

Then came the news! I found out that Jennifer was not hurting for money nor was her mother. In fact, her mother owned several rental properties and had a place at Lake Gaston, Virginia and even a home in Nags Head, North Carolina! According to Jennifer, now I could relax because as long as I could use my good name she could care for the expense. Wow! From a life of an ameba to a trip down easy street which proves "whatever a man is sowing this he shall also reap".

For a number of years, Jennifer's Mom had owned two antique shops and literally made a small fortune. Most of the income was obtained by selling fireworks and in those days there was no shortage of customers. Lorene, Jennifer's Mom, became quite the entrepreneur and added to her stingy ways amassed a nice bundle of cash.

I remember one night; Jennifer was talking plans for the wedding and her mother's concern over cost. Jennifer's response was "that is why you need to get up off some of that green!" Now, I fully understood.

That explained everything. Jennifer's first gift to me was a nine hundred dollar diamond studded ring that really floored me. I was overwhelmed to say the least. Prior to this point, I had only worn silver because frankly, it was all I could afford. Now started my reformation and return to class and I loved it!

The light I found at the end of my tunnel was now shinning

brighter and brighter. In fact, in my first book, *Clown In A Cowboy Hat*, the second poem, Nightmares Are Never Gone, I spoke of that light and from that story came this book. No one could ever had convinced me that after I left the ministry that twenty-one years later I would become a published author!

J. Lee Gilbert

Chapter 29

SEPTEMBER NINETEENTH NINETEEN NINETY- NINE

It was a beautiful Saturday morning on September nineteenth in nineteen ninety nine and Jennifer and I was up early on our way to beautiful Maymont Park in downtown Richmond, Virginia to start the decorations for our wedding. We only had three hours to complete the job and then return home to clean up and wait for the limousine.

Just when it looked like we would not finish in time, my brother Jimmy and his son Joey arrived early and insisted on completing the job. It is sad to think that only three years later, Jimmy would suffer a massive heart attack and pass away. At any rate, due to Jimmy's willingness to assist, we were sure to be on time for what has proved to be the wisest decision of my life!

My brother, Jimmy, was a saint that day! However, together we were quite mischievous. Many times, as kids, and even more so as adults, we found ourselves on the short end of the stick. Our parents often left us alone and that set us free to indulge in trouble. Although innocent, it was just enough to irritate.

When I was nine, Mom and Dad, James and Betty for the

record, had gone somewhere. Jimmy and I played army but with BB guns! We had a ball but in the interim, we killed mom's canary! We left it alone and when Mom returned, we acted like we didn't know what had happened to her bird. However, it did not take long before we were found out and the whip came down!

When we were older and on our own, Jimmy had not changed. In the bars he would have all the girls believing he owned the place. One night, to my surprise, the club owner where we happened to be introduced me to the crowd as a studio musician with a popular band of that day and I ended up on stage playing Johnny B. Goode, lead guitar! When I came off the stage, I swore I was going to kill Jimmy! Actually, I would not have traded the moment for all the tea in China and today I thank God for my brother and miss him dearly. He passed away in September 2002.

By the time we arrived home, the wedding party was in full swing. My son and best man, Kevin; my daughter, Beckie; Kevin's girlfriend and a bride's maid, Sabrina and Jennifer's best friend at the time, Molly who would serve as a bride's maid also made up the wedding party. Finally, there was my grandson, Matthew, who would serve as the ring barrier and needless to say, he made me very proud. Of course, Jennifer's stepfather, Dale would give away the bride. Everyone was on board and we were set for a beautiful September nineteenth wedding day!

Just seventeen years after my illness and battle over child

support, I was about to embark on a new life and soon even a new career although I had no idea at the time. It would be a secret dream revealed and like my new life with Jennifer, it was a road full of pluses.

Ken, Dale and I arrived at the wedding as scheduled. Doctor Winn, the minister, the caterer and the photographers were all in place when the limousine arrived with my beautiful bride to be! I am a bit prejudice but when she came out of the limo it was like an angel arriving to save the day! Everyone watched as the procession began with each bride's maid marching in step followed by my angel.

Looking back, it is hard to phantom those lean years. How could a person live on such a meager income and at the same time live so well? Just when it seemed like I was going down for the third time something would happen to lift me up and back on my feet.

Often times, I would look at a tall stack of bills and a bank account that was nothing short of chump change! Each time I got my check, weekly, due to the state taking sixty six percent for child support, there was nothing left to deposit. However, not willing to concede, I was determined to prove the old adage: where there is a will, there is a way!

I also am very convinced that if we pray for help and then work in harmony with your prayers, God will respond in a positive way.

If there is ever any doubt, remember this story because I am living proof! Always remember, where there is a will there is a way.

It proved to be the greatest moment of my life! When it came time for me to repeat my vows, I chocked up! The words just would not come out but after a long pause I finally was able to say "I do" and we were pronounced "husband and wife". Everyone cheered and for me life was just beginning! "Job" was now going to be rewarded double and the struggle was now worthwhile.

After all the pictures were taken, the reception went into full swing. For me, it was all a done deal with the toast made by my son, Ken, which brought chills to my spine ending with Jennifer and I on the dance floor as everyone cheered. Celine Dion sang Because You Loved Me and as far as I was concerned that moment made the *Unforeseen Occurrence* I had endured all worthwhile.

Finally, the cake was cut and Jennifer tossed the flowers over her shoulder and we were off to prepare for our honeymoon. Everyone started throwing rice but we made it inside the limo although my boss, Joe Lupini, said we cheated and opened the door and everyone began throwing the rice at us while wishing us all the best!

We finally made it home but the race was just beginning as we rushed to get dressed to return and clean up the mess only to find our family and friends had already started the job for us and in fact, were just about finished upon our arrival. After a quick check, we were off to Washington, D.C. where we had a room waiting and a flight scheduled for departure at 6:03 a.m. bound for Atlanta and from there to Acapulco, Mexico!

We arrived in Washington at 1 a.m. and only after three hours of rest, we were up at 4 a.m. and rushing to the airport. Right on schedule we left at 6:03 a.m. and were off to a trip of a lifetime for me! As we flew over our beautiful country I thought, from twenty-one months of disability; nine and a half years of prison, two full time jobs and one more failed marriage, now my life was starting all over one more time but this time for real.

This time with a woman that not only promised me forever but also actually set out to prove it. From the word go, it was obvious that I was finally and truly number one to a beautiful woman. Even Jennifer's Mom assured me, once Jennifer made up her mind a herd of elephants could not change it.

This was one *deadbeat dad* story that was about to prove to the world, there are no reasons to neglect your responsibility and there are no circumstances that you cannot bare in order to prove you do not have to be a *deadbeat dad.* Also, you can be happy if you choose to be.

The results for me were obvious. Now married to the most beautiful woman in the universe and sleeping with a clean conscience, I could not have written the program better myself.

However, the real story was just around the corner and

amazingly, it had been unfolding for years and I never realized it's value until the moment it came to light. The Bible clearly states: "*Unforeseen Occurrence* befall us all"!

Chapter 30

THE TRIP OF A LIFE TIME

To actually fly over Mexico and to witness an active volcano is truly an all inspiring experience. Neither of us had ever seen such a sight and it proved to be a moment neither of us would forget. Actually, there were many *Unforeseen Occurrences* about to take place that neither of us will ever forget.

Fortunately for Jennifer, she did not get much rest so for most of the flight she was asleep. She is so beautiful but airplanes and heights are not her forte'. The flight was smooth and without incident and almost like transferring from the world to heaven and what a feeling!

Due to our lack of preparation, the first problem we encountered was currency. Upon our arrival, the Mexican people were on us like white on rice for money. We thought they were so nice but in reality they were money hungry! In Mexico a dollar was worth nine times more than what we thought and so when we tipped the baggage man three dollars in realty I gave him a twenty seven dollar tip. What a fool!

I continued to throw money away all the way to the motel. We were very hungry upon our arrival at the Hyatt Motel and made a beeline to the restaurant only to discover the average cost of a meal was a hundred and forty dollars! We left the motel and ventured across the street while money hungry Mexicans followed us all the way offering all sorts of help in an effort to obtain the all mighty dollar. At the Wal-Mart we ended up at, there was a Burger King but reality set in right away when we saw the cost of a large sandwich was twenty-three dollars! By this time, Jennifer was near panic! Throughout the store the prices were outrageous and even a jar of peanut butter was twenty-one dollars!

We settled for some dried up fried chicken and some hard rolls and sat down in despair to eat. When it came time to pay we went ballistic! Jennifer walked through the store shouting if there was anyone in the store that could speak English? Finally, a lady came forth to help although her English was very poor. When it was all said and done, we thought they had cheated themselves nine fold but by this time felt justified and not guilty because we had gone through pure hell.

We had given the lady a twenty-dollar bill for the meal and she gave us one hundred and sixty dollars in change! As wrong as the thought may have seemed, I was ready for retribution and felt some degree of satisfaction although the last laugh would be on me.

We returned to our rooms very tired; discouraged and ready to go back home when a representative of the Mexican government called our room. He emphasized the need not to venture out until we talked because it was important we understood a few things. Now he tells us! Shortly thereafter, we were in his office amazed at his explanation of the Mexican currency and exchange. When we left his office, we had a new mood and new attitude ready to start our honeymoon with renewed vigor! What a relief.

After a good night's rest, we were up and ready for a hardy breakfast. The meal was great and the price just right. Needless to say, I really over did it.

Now it was time to make a fool out of myself and yet have a ball with the most beautiful woman in the universe in my opinion.

We went down to the motel pool where I planned to show off my manly body! Months earlier, Jennifer's Mom had made, at my request, what I called a normal men's swimsuit. In my opinion, today, men's swimsuits look like parachutes. My suit was white, tight and fit just right! I would have looked great but I failed to put it on correctly. In fact, I put it on inside out! After about fifteen minutes on the beach, Jennifer noticed my mistake and the laughter began. I made it to the restroom like a bat out of hell to change and even today we are still laughing about the event. I guess I'll never live it down. Even published authors are human and capable of making mistakes.

There were many highlights during our honeymoon in Mexico but probably the most notable were the cliff divers. We were able to film the whole event and it serves as a warm keepsake to say the least.

After seven days in Mexico, we were ready to depart carrying many fond memories. However, there were more *Unforeseen Occurrences* over the horizon, some of which were not so pleasant but proved to be valuable lessons that have molded my life into what I have wanted from the beginning.

During our trip home we had to change planes in Atlanta. However, upon our arrival there we had to sit on the plane for almost forty-five minutes because there was a mechanical problem with another flight on the landing field that was blocking incoming flights. We were finally rushed to the next flight only to discover with the delay our baggage did not make the flight with us. Upon our arrival in Richmond, Virginia there was no luggage and the nightmare began trying to locate it. We returned home early on Saturday but did not receive our suitcases until late Sunday and Jennifer had almost worried herself sick because of her expensive jewelry. We were glad to get it back so we could resume a normal life again free from worry.

Not so fast! That same Sunday morning I discovered someone had shattered the glass on my pickup truck and I was furious! It was obvious to me that a vendetta was still being paid but I found comfort in the Biblical promise: "whatever a man is sowing this he shall also reap"! I was sure who was responsible and knew she would have to repay in kind! My return to a wholesome life style had begun, thank God!

The truck was soon repaired and paid for by my insurance and it was back to normal in no time. My happiness created by Jennifer, over shadowed the ugly that were created by another woman and it did not bother me at all. In fact, the joys I was about to face far out weighed any bad that was to come too.

Although the ramifications of the brain hemorrhage was long gone and behind me, the child support issues resolved, the lessons learned were indubitably etched in my memory forever! Even today Jennifer and I often talk about it. If you are a male with children or just thinking about marriage, then I suggest you think seriously about all the possibilities and not just about the beautiful girl you are about to marry. Remember, the commitment is for a lifetime!

Therefore, before making the commitment, calculate the cost. Have I accomplished all my goals? Is this truly the person I wish to spend the rest of my life? Believe me, if you have wondering eyes or even the slightest doubt, reconsider, because hindsight is always twenty-twenty and is always too late. Remember too, you cannot turn back the hands of time. Marriage should be viewed as a lifetime commitment. Failed marriages often times produce *deadbeat dads!*

J. Lee Gilbert

Chapter 31

DREAM HOUSE

I never believed after my illness, that life could be so good! Jennifer and my grand Creator proved me wrong because, like Job, my life was just beginning.

The first thing on the agenda was our new house. From the word go, almost every day, we went to the construction site to ensure the work was being performed to our specifications and it was great! Our desire was to have an all black and white house, inside and out, when all was said and done. Until this very day, I am in total awe over the ownership of my own house and often am found outside or inside admiring our accomplishment.

After my illness and nine plus years of two full time jobs, I had no idea of ever owning another home. *Deadbeat dads* have no clue what they are missing out on!

The house included overhead black ceiling fans and even my favorite black toilets. The construction workers seemed to love it and as a result seemed to take special interest in our house. The problems that developed were not with construction but more so with the company in charge of the whole project. It seemed like every day they were calling to request a monetary adjustment and usually for more money. Finally, in total frustration, I telephoned the company and in no uncertain terms told them never to call again especially if it was about more money! To our surprise, the calls stopped and we were back to enjoying the prospect of a new home again as it was being built.

My suggestion to any would be home buyers is to steer clear of planned communities that are run, controlled or operated by an association! Truly it can be a nightmare! Even today after all is said and done, basically, we pay two mortgages, one to the mortgage company and one to the association. What a rip off! What is more, we reap no rewards for our payment to the association but we do it for peace and to be left alone. The only benefits we believe is the trash pick up or when I hound them enough for a service I'm suppose to already receive.

In the end, we had two final fights with what I referred to in the finality, as the Gestapo! In my community, there were several colors of doors and matching shutters. Of course, we wanted black but the construction management company had us scheduled for an ugly green and we vehemently opposed and went before the board to argue our case and we won! Seems the house across the street had black shutters but had not been sold and they simply traded off to our relief and of course for an additional one hundred dollars! Imagine that!

Finally, we discovered there was a large drain placed in front of our house and in our front yard. Needless to say, it was an eye sore and an invitation for all sorts of trouble. It took almost a year and a half of pure hell to get it corrected. On the day it was complete was pretty much the end of our troubles with the management company to this day. In fact, they've become very cooperative and we believe they finally realize we are here to make the community better and not to cause them heartaches.

Later there was some trouble with the Homeowner's Association over my company truck, a commercial vehicle, being parked at my house. It seems the covenants of the community would not permit such marked automobiles and I was forced to use decal covers! However, a few weeks later, Jennifer and I were told of another decaled truck in the community, which in fact was one of the community association's own trucks. I took pictures of it and sent them to the community management personnel with a note asking: "What's wrong with this picture?" They soon backed off and to this day we've not been bothered by that association!

I guess the best part was the finale! My boss and very good friend, Joe Lupini, came to my rescue again! First of all, his company did the pre-treat on my new home at no cost to protect it from termites. When it came time to move, Joe allowed all his employees and the use of his trucks to make the move and it was great because it was all done in a half of a day!

It was on December twenty ninth nineteen ninety-nine when we closed and moved in before the expected computer crash of two thousand that never occurred. Instead of a crash we smoothly landed into marital bliss, the greatest moment of my life and the *Unforeseen Occurrence* I had hoped for all my life. However, that was only the beginning.

Chapter 32

TESTED AND WORTHY TO CARRY THE TORCH

Jennifer discovered that her new husband was multifaceted but one talent that could not go unnoticed. Writing!

When my vision returned after my illness, I had to learn how to read and write all over again. It was then that I returned to writing poetry. During my nine and a half years of two full time jobs trying to avoid a *deadbeat dad* status that I often referred to as my prison sentence, at night, I wrote a lot of poetry. For every experience I had it was followed by some poetic pros.

Often the International Library of Poetry encouraged me to assimilate my own book but I pretty much ignored their efforts mainly because of expense. In my mind's eye, it would cost a fortune and I knew nothing about the book business. To me it was just a scam to get money. However, when Jennifer discovered my work and the letters from the International Library of Poetry, she began to encourage me to pursue the book idea and so I began to formulate my first book. It was in October of two thousand I began to collect my work together for what proved to be my first completed book.

Actually, a few years earlier, I had tried to do a book but it was way off course. It was called *The Words Of An Outlaw* but it was too much material and looked more like an encyclopedia than a poetry book. Basically, it was just an attractive notebook. It had no copyright; no ISBN number; no table of contents and no bar code, just to mention a few of the imperfections. Frankly, I was just learning. It was truly amateurish to say the least.

After I reduced its' contents and changed the title it was still just a binder with no table of contents and none of those details previously mentioned. The artwork was all that of the Author and believe me, I am no artist by any stretch of the imagination! However, at least the idea was there and just needed some serious polishing.

For years I had thought of myself as a *Clown In A Cowboy Hat* and decided that would be the title of my first book. It was full of bitterness, love and to say the least sarcasm the reader would have it easy understanding my plight. However, the outcome would be a positive one as I described in poetry my journey through life culminating in heavenly bliss with Jennifer.

In reading *Clown In A Cowboy Hat*, the reader will discover deep-rooted spirituality with constant quotes and reference to the scriptures. After all, it's the book I started my career on and it is the book my writing is based.

Let it be known to all, writing a book is the easy part compared to getting it published and into the bookstores. In fact, it is easier to get a camel through the eye of a needle than to get a company to review and accept your book. After a long and exhausting effort, only to end in failure to get that accomplished, Jennifer and I decided to open our own publishing company.

Since for years, I have always referred to myself as the king of hearts and even had a tattoo reading: The King of Hearts and even referred to Jennifer as my Queen of Hearts, we decided to call our Company, King and Queen Publishers, Inc.

After several failed attempts, finally in October of two thousand one Barnes and Nobles accepted my material and by December my books, by now I had two, were accepted and would begin to appear in the stores slowly. My second book had also been accepted just three days before our first official signing at Barnes and Nobles and it was called: *You Can't Judge A Book By It's Cover* and to date it proves to be our best seller.

In that book, *You Can't Judge A Book By It's Cover*, you will find many references and quotes from the Bible, a book I encourage *Deadbeat Dads* to consider and for that matter all people that wish to clean up their life and way of thinking. In fact on page seven of the book, *You Can't Judge A Book By It's Cover*, people are warned to read between the lines because there were many hidden and subliminal messages.

In August of that same year, Ms. Angela Agee of Barnes and Nobles scheduled us as a part of a new writer's night event along with Willie Tee who wrote *Winds Of Destiny;* Marigold Fields who wrote *A Long Journey Home* and I was on my way! That evening, only eight days after 911, I sold and signed fifteen books and we were in heaven! One week earlier, at a business meeting of the Central Virginia Pest Management Association, I had sold twenty-four and I felt on top of the world!

Finally, we were realizing a dream come true. From those early signings, when we had no clue what was expected, we have gradually matured into true professionals and loving every minute of it! Almost weekly, there is a bookstore I am scheduled to appear and to autograph books. Jennifer and I welcome each signing with open arms and are always forty-five or more minutes early at each signing.

The highlight of our career and life together was my successful effort to appear on television with a group of authors. I approached channel twelve's call 12 Coordinator, Bonnie Talbert, about a writer's night in which the public would be invited to call in and ask the professional authors how to get published. My idea went over like a lead balloon. At the time, Bonnie just did not believe there was a market out there to generate enough calls. However, she did request a letter detailing my idea and she would consider it for a later time. For future writers trying to promote their own book, I here present that original letter sent to Bonnie Talbert at N.B.C. Channel 12:

Ms. Bonnie Talbert

Channel 12

12 On Your Side

Dear Ms. Bonnie Talbert:

April is National Poetry Mouth, which would be an appropriate time to host a local writer's question and answer panel on your Call 12 programs.

The individuals that would make up the panel would include representative & Community Relations Manager from Barnes & Nobles Bookstores, Ms. Angela Agee; Nick Mangieri, Author; Marigold Fields, Author; Willie Tee, Author and J. Lee Gilbert, published Author.

Each of the panelists will be prepared to answer questions such as:

1. How can I get started in writing my own book?

2. Who can help me get my work published?

3. What are the steps to self-publishing?

4. What organizations will review your manuscript?

5. What publications can I read for publishing ideas?

6. What cost might I incur in having my book published?

7. Why are Author autograph sessions at bookstores and libraries, a great way to get information from the Authors?

Please call J. Lee Gilbert with King & Queen Publishers Inc. at 762-7177 or at 833-3777 with a date and we will prepare the panel.

Thank you for your time and consideration.

After some time for deliberation, the call came to inform me the idea was accepted. Now the ball was in my court and I was calling the shots, so to speak. The television station wanted the program right away but I chose to delay for the National Poetry Month of April, which was several months down the pike. Reluctantly, the station accepted and I began to put the wheels in motion for a successful event. The program was slated for April eighth, two thousand and two. It was indeed the beginning of great things for King & Queen Publishers, Inc. the name of our new company.

It would turn out to be a perfect choice because it was National Poetry month and I was a poet! Needless to say, we were elated and felt on top of the world. We got busy promoting the event, which included the public libraries and all the Barnes and Nobles stores possible. Before everything was said and done; Author, J. Lee Gilbert; King & Queen Publishers Inc. and our first three books were becoming available nationwide. From the public libraries to the national archives libraries and the major book chains, my books were becoming commonplace.

Getting into the public libraries was not as easy as we were led to believe. In fact, to all would be writers and future authors, do not believe the libraries are an easy sale. The successes we have realized have only been local, in other words, only in the communities in which I live have the libraries been friendly and willing to promote my writings. Thank God for them.

After the successful call 12-segment television show, we were invited back for another event! After the show, I had to appear at a Barnes & Nobles store and the support of the public was much changed. In fact, I signed twenty-eight books that day, the best signing I have had to date and all because of the television program.

Since that night, there have been two additional television shows each even more successful than the one before. In fact, our last show to date, April seventeenth, two thousand and three, we got one hundred ninety seven phone calls in just one hour and twenty minutes! Even Barnes & Noble included pictures from the show in their company magazine.

The signings kept coming and my nightmare and *Unforeseen Occurrence* had become blissful! Like the Biblical Job, my tenacity and desire to be steadfast and true after many years at the bottom, began to reverse itself. Without any effort my entire road to disaster became one full of successes.

If anyone were to approach me and ask, if given the opportunity, would I do it all over again, my response would be a resounding yes! From my departure from the ministry, through the brain hemorrhage and my up hill climb back to a successful career as an author, I believe everyone has control of their own destiny and can decide to be happy or sad, successful or a failure. After nineteen eighty-two and my illness, I came to realize I could do anything I chose and when I wanted with a lot of positive thinking and faith in God. Truly as Jesus stated: "That expression, 'If I can', why all things are possible if you have faith" or if you *think* you can! The *Unforeseen Occurrences* in your life are simply tests to see if you are worthy to carry the *torch*. I wish you *God speed!*

ABOUT THE AUTHOR

J. Lee Gilbert was born in 1949. After his formal education he became a full-time minister and public speaker for eleven years. Finding it very difficult to help those that did not want help, J. Lee left the ministry only to suffer a brain hemorrhage and stroke and the ordeal lasted twenty-one months. For the final eleven months of the ordeal, J. Lee was blind which was noted in the New England Journal of Medicine because in nineteen eighty-two left handed people did not survive cerebral hemorrhages.

Miraculously, his vision began to return, only to discover he could no longer read or write and had to learn all over again. During that process he wrote three books of poetry and Co-Authored twenty books of poetry with such organizations as the International Library of Poetry, the New York Poetry Guild and the Sparrowgrass Poetry Forum. Now he releases this book explaining the struggle and his determination not to be a deadbeat dad! Finally, if a person makes up his mind, he does not have to fail and can actually build a legacy for others to emulate.

September 19, 1999